POWER POLITICS IN HARYANA

POWER POLITICS IN HARYANA

A View from the Bridge

BHIM S. DAHIYA

GYAN

Published by

Gyan Publishing House
5, Ansari Road
Daryaganj, New Delhi-110002
Phone: 011-47034999, 9811692060
E-mail: books@gyanbooks.com

Distribution Network
gyanbooks.com
India, USA, Canada, UK, Australia, France

ISBN: 978-81-212-1007-2 (HB)

Reprint in India, 2024
First Published, 2008

Printed at: Gyan Press, Delhi.

Power Politics in Haryana: A View from the Bridge
Author: Bhim S. Dahiya

DEDICATED

To the Late Ch. Hardwari Lal,
Who Estranged me from the Academy
and
To the Late Dr. Sarup Singh, who Inducted me into Politics

Contents

Preface

After the release early this year of my semi-political book, *Dr. Sarup Singh and His Times,* the larger narrative of Haryana politics, of which Dr. Sarup Singh was only a stray reveler, started pressing for a release from memory. What initially started as a trickle soon turned into a regular stream, pouring out account after account of persons and events I had known and heard in my lifetime. Once the spontaneous flow had completed its run I thought of certain writers of local histories and practioners of politics who could confirm or mend the recalls I had recorded in the manuscript of this book. Reading through local histories and interacting with sober politicians added to the manuscript the much-needed facts and figures which made the narrative more sharp and substantial.

Although based on historical events and public personalities, the narrative of the present book has not been rendered from the viewpoint of a professional historian. Since the book is focused on episodes and anecdotes, persons and personalities, it carries the qualities more of a literary work than those of a typical history. The author's interest in telling stories rather than record events, draw portraits, rather than trace patterns will be found to mark the book's style. Not that trends and tendencies, analyses and inferences are not a part of the narrative. All *that* is also there. But greater emphasis falls on what constitutes the 'human' in all that flows in the running stream of the long narrative. In other words, it is the poetry of politics, poetry both comic and tragic, lyrical and discordant, which predominates over the factual and the database.

Scientific objectivity may be desirable in the reporting of political events and drawing of political portraits, but this virtue is bound to take away from the narrative the pleasure readers naturally derive from episodes and anecdotes designed to address emotions and feelings, ideas and ideals that mankind is accustomed to live by. Without any attempt, therefore, to deliberately distort or consciously concoct things concerning historical events or political personages, the narrative has been keyed to the human note. In the analysis and interpretation of affairs involving men and women, only a reasonable measure of objectivity is decidedly present all through the book, including the portions personally involving the author as a political personage.

Like any normal human being the author may not be wholly free from individual prejudices and preferences, but it can be said with certainty that he has tried hard not to permit any such weakness to spoil the authenticity of an event or the integrity of an individual. No doubt, the author, while in active politics himself, had rivals and adversaries, companions and collaborators, outside as well as inside his own political party. But with long experience as a social and literary critic he has had the reputation of being an objective commentator on both men and matters. All care has been taken to give all political figures their due, with firm intent to neither slight nor bloat any one's general reputation registered in popular perception.

Making no claim to historical accuracy, the book only promises to offer 'a view from the bridge' of Haryana's power politics as it has come down to us from its inception in the era of Ch. Chhotu Ram to its present phase in the regime of Ch. Bhupinder Singh Hooda. As is usual with the author, the narrative must interest readers, involve them in the matter and the manner of narration, impart to them knowledge of the subject, and compel them to contemplate not only the particulars but also the universals relating to the affairs of mankind. The Haryanvi touch both in the anecdotes as well as in its culture-specific humour has been maintained throughout. Last of all, the author would be ready to apologise to whoever finds anything less than fair in relation to his person or party to which he belongs. Castes and communities have been discussed wherever unavoidable, but with utmost care to make a true representation of each and all.

Digressions, of course, are unavoidable in any narrative concerning the affairs of men. The present narrative, even while its subject is power politics, has, after all, human affairs to reckon with. As such, it is but natural that digressions would creep into it as and when the opportunity arose. As Jonathan Swift, the English satirist of the eighteenth century, remarked, 'without digression, there is no great progression'. William Blake, the pioneer of the Romantic Movement, had thought that 'without contraries is no progression'. Both thinkers are not far from the truth. For digression and contradiction, after all, are contrary to decision or determination. Thus, in our narrative about the affairs of those engaged in the business of power politics, it was just not possible to have avoided the entry of the inevitable. As we know, digressions are as natural to the art of story telling as the sweet juice is to the growth of watermelons.

Just as the present work was inevitable as the political follow-up of my earlier book—*Dr. Sarup Singh and His Times*-so is inevitable as the educational follow-up of that very book my next work — *Higher Education is Haryana*. These three books are not only interrelated, but are also complementary to each other. As the present one is appearing in about a year's time after the first one, so will the next one follow in about the same time hereafter. These three books are, in a sense, three volumes on the growth of modern Haryana politically, educationally, culturally. This growth is, of course, viewed in the related and larger contexts of the country and the continent, of which the small but significant state of Haryana has been a part.

Bhim S. Dahiya

Acknowledgements

Although largely a recall from my memory, this book is not an exclusive edifice; it is indebted in ample measure to various writers of local and regional histories as well as to several persons of political significance. I owe my sincere thanks to Dr. Ranjit Singh, whose book on Professor Sher Singh provided a good deal of information on the political proceedings in Punjab as they culminated in the creation of the present - day states of Haryana and Punjab. I am also grateful to Dr. Nonika Datta, whose book *Forming Identity: A Social History of the Jats* gave me insight into the rise of the Jats as a political force in the region now named Haryana. I owe my thanks also to Dr. M.M. Juneja whose various books on Hisar, especially *The Diaries of Dr. Ramji Lal Hooda* and *Hisar City: Places and Personalities* made available valuable facts about certain relevant political figures of the district. My thanks are also due to Shiva N.Malik, whose book on Seth Chhaju Ram is intimately related to the political history of Haryana.

In the shaping of this book, the most significant contribution came from Ch. Bhupinder Singh Hooda, the present Chief Minister of Haryana, who suggested an extension of the book's canvas from the original account of forty years, that is, the period after the creation of Haryana on November 1, 1966, to the present larger narrative, which begins with the foundation of Haryana politics in the early years of the twentieth century. I am also grateful to Professor Sher Singh, with whom I had long conversations which yielded useful knowledge about the people and politics of Punjab and Haryana. I am indepted to Dr. Subhas Chander for a valuable addition to the narration. My thanks are also due to Sh. Arvind Chaudhary, a grandson of Seth Chhaju Ram, Ch. Shyam Chand, Ch. Tajiner Singh Maan, and Sh. Ranbir Singh who also offered useful information on some of the facts recorded in the book.

I must mention here my gratitude to my wife, children and grandchildren whose love and affection have kept me firmly committed to the goals I assigned myself. My wife, Sudesh, my son, Tribhuvan, my daughters, Divya and Hema, my daughter-in-law, Suman, and my grandsons, Siddharth and Rohiteshwar, are all so caring and affectionate that I cannot ask for more.

I owe, last of all, special thanks to Professor R.W. Desai who read through the manuscript and removed many an embarrassing oddities of grammar and punctuation.

Bhim S. Dahiya

Abbreviations

AJGAR	-	Ahirs, Jats, Gujars, Rajputs
BKD	-	Bharatiya Kisan Dal
BLD	-	Bharatiya Lok Dal
INLD	-	Indian National Lok Dal
LD	-	Lok Dal
RLD	-	Rashtriya Lok Dal
CPI	-	Communist Party of India
CPI (M)	-	Communist Party of India (Marxist)
BJP	-	Bharatiya Janata Party
JD(S)	-	Janata Dal (Secular)
JD (U)	-	Janata Dal (United)
RJD	-	Rashtriya Janata Dal
SP	-	Samajwadi Party
U.P.	-	Uttra Pradesh

1

The Roots in Rohtak 1916-1945

Haryana politics as we know it today can be said to have started in the early years of the twentieth century with the launching of Ch. Chhotu Ram's weekly called *Jat Gazette* in 1916. In response to this was launched Pandit Sri Ram Sharma's *Haryana Tilak* in 1923. While both these weeklies were published from Rohtak, the home district of their editors, the two represented the two poles of Haryana politics, originally raised by these leaders but continued by their successors right into our own times. Both Ch. Chhotu Ram and Pandit Sri Ram Sharma emerged as local caste leaders respectively of Jats and Brahmans, emerging at the same time important regional leaders of the Unionist Party and the Congress Party.

Using their political mouthpieces (their weeklies) for furthering their respective interests of regional and national politics, these two leaders set up two broad polarities of political consciousness among the people of Haryana, promoting the caste divide between Jats and Brahmans and the nationalist divide between opponents and supporters of the Congress Party. The other castes gathered around these two poles, with the landed peasantry siding with Ch. Chhotu Ram and the business and trading castes siding with Pandit Sri Ram Sharma.

It is interesting to note that despite their local political rivalry with the Brahmans, considered to have dominance in the Congress Party, the Jats of Haryana, more than any other caste or community, became the staunch followers of Maharishi Dayanand Saraswati's Arya Samaj, although the Maharishi was a Brahman! The Brahmans, on the contrary, became staunch opponents of the Arya Samaj, being anti-idolatory, whereas idolatory for most non-landed Brahmans was an occupation, a means of livelihood.

The Arya Samaj had got a foothold in Haryana with the opening of its branches in the 1880's at Hisar and Rohtak. With both these branches was associated one of the leading Jat families of Haryana from the village of Sanghi in Rohtak district; the two brothers of this family, Dr. Ramji Lal and Ch. Matu Ram, were important founding members of the Arya Samaj in Haryana. A grandson of Ch. Matu Ram Hooda, Ch. Bhupinder Singh Hooda*, is now the Chief Minister of Haryana. To the subsequent generations of the family we shall return later; for the present, we need to look into the role of these first-generation leaders of an important political family of modern Haryana.

* It need to be stated here that whereas the Jat leaders until as late as the formation of Haryana did not use their *gotra* (sub-caste), the present-day Jat leaders invariably use it. Bhupinder Singh Hooda is the third-generation leader of the family who started using his last name.

The Hooda family of Sanghi invited the wrath of Snatani and Puranic Brahmans as well as of the traditional Jats who organized panchyats of the Jat khaps and the Hindu communities to pronounce the boycott of Dr. Ramji Lal and Ch. Matu Ram, both having converted to the new sect of the Arya Samaj. Undaunted by the conservative threats, the two brothers went ahead to spread the message of the new religious order, providing leadership to the new converts who were being bullied by the forces of blind faith. With these strong Jat leaders coming to the fore, the Arya Samaj movement got accelerated and soon became a dominant sect in the rural areas having a Jat majority. These leaders established *gausalas* and *gurukals*, which soon became the resource-centers for spreading the Arya Samaj movement. In the 1880's, the Arya Samaj also created its branches in the present-day districts of Karnal, Jind, Sirsa, etc., mostly in areas with a strong Jat presence.

The enlightened and reformist work of this Hooda family of Sanghi is laudable, indeed. In keeping with the crusade of Swami Dayanand for widow remarriage, and in keeping with his own enlightened conscience, Dr. Ramji Lal became the first willful man among the Jats to marry a widow. In 1905, in his *Diaries*, he wrote the following about a widow he had met on a visit to another village:

> She had a male child from her earlier marriage. She is very poor. She is of good character and conduct. She is not ugly looking. I saw her with her mother at Barahi. I would like her to be my wife in case I do not find anything that goes against her. (Juneja and More, 45)

This bold step brought a revolution in the community of Jats in particular, whose members in large numbers died during the wars, leaving their widows in great social and financial distress. Dr. Ramji Lal's role as a committed social reformer and a respectable Jat leader also included active participation in managing orphanages, schools, sabhas, etc., and his contribution towards keeping his community united, often marred by clan conflicts between Deswali and Baagari Jats. He always brokered peace between warring factions, being a detached and saintly person whom all revered.

Thus, the Hooda family of Sanghi acquired a social and religious status, raising it above the rest in Rohtak and Hisar districts, becoming influential even in other districts surrounding these two. For its firm commitment to the Arya Samaj, to the Congress Party, and to community service, the family enjoys a distintion to which not many can lay as strong a claim. That the family's commitments have remained unslackened for over a century shows the fine metal the family is made of.

With his elite education from the Medical College, Lahore, receiving his MBBS degree in 1886, Dr. Ramji Lal joined as Assistant Civil Surgeon at Hisar in 1892, and became a leading member of the Arya Samaj in Haryana. He came to acquire such an influence in the Jat community that even the tall leaders of Rothak and Hisar like Ch. Chhotu Ram, Ch. Tika Ram, Ch. Matu Ram, Ch. Chhaju Ram and Ch. Fateh Singh became Arya Samajis receiving inspiration from him.

However, while Dr. Ramji Lal devoted himself to the spiritual and social uplift of the people of Haryana, the Jats in particular, his other brother, Ch. Matu Ram Hooda, became the third plank of Haryana politics in the Rohtak region, with the other two represented by Ch. Chhotu Ram and Pandit Sri Ram Sharma. As we shall see later, the politics of Rothak in particular, and of Haryana in general, was determined and symbolized by these three pillars.

Another pioneering work the Hooda family of Sanghi launched was the establishment of the Jat Anglo-Sanskrit High School at Rohtak in 1914 with Ch. Matu Ram as its founder President. Later, Ch. Lal Chand and Ch. Chhotu Ram started another school named Jat Heroes Memorial High School and became, respectively, the President and the Secretary of its Management. The two schools were then merged in 1926 as a result of mediation by Seth Chhaju Ram and Dr. Ramji Lal, under an agreement signed by Ch. Matu Ram, Ch. Chhotu Ram, Ch. Lal Chand, Seth Chhaju Ram and Dr. Ramji Lal. The new name given to the school was the Jat Heroes Memorial Anglo-Sasnkrit High School. It was this school that became a centre and a site for the contesting Jat leaders who sought recognition in the community through the politics of its Management. Those who came out of this school had a strong sense of being Jats and an equally strong zeal to serve the community.

As the Indian Freedom Struggle accelerated in the early twentieth century, especially during World War I, the politics of Rohtak and the rest of Haryana started taking shape. With Ch. Lal Chand and Ch. Chhotu Ram drifting towards the Empire, both getting involved in the recruitment of soldiers for the World War, increasing the number of recruits in Rohtak alone from 6,245 in 1915 to 22,144 in 1918 (Datta, 91), those on the Congress side like Ch. Matu Ram and Pandit Sri Ram Sharma took a strong stand against the Unionist Party. Thus, the battle lines for the power politics in Haryana were drawn around this time.

Ch. Chhotu Ram, more smart than Ch. Lal Chand, as also with greater popularity among the Jats, extended his area of political activity into western U.P. and Rajasthan and tried to activate the Jat community against the money-lenders and their associates in the British administration. Ch. Chhotu Ram, like most Jat leaders, combined the twin allegiance to his caste and to his faith (the Arya Samaj). The British detested his 'fanaticism' in this passionate task he pursued. But the upliftment of the Jats, his 'race', had become the mission of his life. He however explained his case as also that of his 'race', characterizing it as different from the Arya Samaj of the urban Hindu, to the satisfaction of the rulers.

Like the other Haryana leaders, such as Ch. Matu Ram and Pandit Sri Ram Sharma, Ch. Chhotu Ram also started his political career in the Congress, remaining the President of Rohtak District Congress Committee between 1916 and 1920. He resigned from the party in 1920, alleging that the Congress was dominated by the upper-caste urbanites, leaving no room for addressing the problems of the poor ruralites, especially the peasantry. For this cause of his Kaum he sacrificed the nationalist politics symbolisded by the Congress and never felt sorry for having done that.

Thus came up yet another plank in Haryana politics: the antagonism between the urban and the rural, or the town and the country. This antagonism gradually came to be represented by the opposition between the Congress and the Unionist Party in Punjab. Through his hard work, Ch. Chhotu Ram gathered around him a gigantic following spread over Haryana, Rajasthan, and western U.P., combining the interests of the Jat community and the Arya Samaj, creating a solid support-base for his politics. Later, he extended this base to include the Sikh and Muslim peasantery of Punjab, culminating at last into the founding of the Unionist Party in 1923.

The Unionist Party, largely consisting of the *zamindars* or peasant proprietors, both big and small, emerged eventually as the ruling outfit in Punjab. Ch. Chhotu Ram went about the task of uniting the entire peasantry of Punjab untired and undaunted, floating the idea of AJGAR, a united force of peaseantry combining the castes of Ahirs (Yadvas), Jats, Gujars and Rajputs, which worked very well, making him an undisputed leader of the rural peasantry all over the undivided Punjab.

In the 1923 election to the Punjab Legislative Council, in which the Unionist Party secured seven out of eight seats of the Haryana region, with Ch. Chhotu Ram and Ch. Lal Chand returned from the constituencies of the rural Rohtak area. In this election, Ch. Lal Chand was opposed by the Congress Swaraj Party candidate, Ch. Matu Ram of village Sanghi. The latter was defeated allegedly by foul means of rigging adopted by the winning candidate. In a historical legal fight, Ch. Matu Ram won the case. The Hon'ble Judges made some sharp observations, such as the following:

> It is inconceivable that any candidate, who wished to keep his hands perfectly clean, would have thought of employing a man of the type of Tek Ram for furthering his election. This fact shows beyond doubt that the Respondent was not scrupulous about the selection of his agent, and if he was not scrupulous about the selection of his agent, would it be surprising if his attitude was the same with respect to the choice of his means. (Narain, 169)

Later, Ch. Chhotu Ram succeeded Ch. Lal Chand to the ministerial position of his predecessor. It is important to note here that the business of rigging is not new in our electoral system, that it has been a part of the political culture in our country, or anywhere for that matter, ever since the democratic elections were initiated. The powerful ones have always resorted to rigging wherever they deemed it necessary. Thanks to the present-day Election Commission of India, this evil practice is getting effectively checked.

The fight that Ch. Matu Ram took up against the mighty Jat leaders of the Unionist Party having a government of their own, backed by the British Raj, was more representative than individual. Between the two planks of politics represented by Ch. Chhotu Ram and Pandit Sri Ram Sharma, marking the antagonisms between the Jats and the Brahman-Banias, between the rural and the urban interests, and between the casteist and the nationalist sentiments, there came to be raised the third pillar by persons like Ch. Matu Ram Hooda who, though Jat by caste, were committed to the larger nationalist politics represented by the Congress Swatantra Party. This third plank of Haryna's power politics was marked by secular rather than sectarian allegiance, by national rather than regional or casteist commitments. Ready to resist the temptations of power and undaunted by the muscle power of the majority, people like Ch. Matu Ram Hooda stood for superior values of the nationalist Congress Party and the reformist Arya Samaj.

Besides Ch. Matu Ram and Pandit Sri Ram Sharma, there were also other important leaders with the same allegiance and commitment to the Congress ideology, such as Ch. Samar Singh (tauntingly called a Pandit), who later got elected to the Punjab Assembly on the Congress ticket in 1952, and Rai Bahadur Ch. Bans Gopal, both from Karnal district, who, too, contested on the Congress Swaraj Party ticket during the pre-Independence period and remained MLA/MLC for years. Ch.

Bans Gopal's family became a noted political centre of Jats just as did Ch. Matu Ram's. Incidentally, the two families got related through the marriage of Dr. Ramji Lal's daughter to Ch. Bans Gopal.

The family of Ch. Bans Gopal had in succession Ch. Randhir Singh, a leading advocate of Karnal who dominated the cooperative activities in Karnal district, including the creation of the Co-operative Sugar Mill at Panipat, and the Cooperative Bank at Karnal and other places. His son, Ch. Surjit Singh, remained an MLA between 1968 and 1977, and also a Minister for some years. The next generation of the family is represented by Ch. Tajinder Singh Maan, who has been an MLA and a Minister between 1991 and 1996 and is again an independent MLA elected in 2005 from the constituency of Pai (in Kaithal district).

Although most Jat leaders came under the influence of Ch. Chhotu Ram and joined the Unionist Party, several Jat leaders, besides the Hoodas of Sanghi, joined the nationalist movement and became members of the Congress Party. A prominent leader, also a staunch Arya Samaji, who came into the limelight a little later, is Professor Sher Singh. As for those from other castes, particularly the Brahmans and Banias, there were numerous leaders in Hisar alone, such as Babu Chura Mani, Lala Lajpat Rai, Pandit Jawahar Lal Bhargva, Babu Jugal Kishor, etc, who actively participated in the country's Freedom Struggle under the banner of the Congress Party.

Here, two things need to be noted: one, that these prominent Jats like Ch. Matu Ram and Ch. Bans Gopal could hold the British Raj titles like those of Zailder and Rai Bahadur and yet at the same time join the Congress Swaraj Party to which Ch. Chhotu Ram and Ch. Lal Chand were opposed; two, that they could remain staunch Arya Smaj leaders as well as comrades in the Congress Party dominated by the Brahmans who viewed the Arya Smaj as a detractor of their orthodox Hindu faith.

Interestingly, whichever political party the Jat leaders chose to join, they remained united in their common pursuit as crusaders of the community and ardent supporters of the Arya Samaj. In other words, these prominent Jat families, while pursuing different political interests, remained united as a community of Jats and Arya Samajis – a neat separation of social and political domains.

It is no less interesting to note that the caste brotherhood was so strong among these leaders that their political or religious affiliations could never weaken it. A revealing instance of this is Ch. Chhotu Ram's message from Lahore to Seth Chhaju Ram in Calcutta that Sardar Bhagat Singh's stay at the latter's residence in 1928 had come to the knowledge of the British authorities and that the young man should be shifted to some unknown place in the city. It also reveals that although both the Jat leaders, famous in their respective areas of politics and business, even while remaining a part of the Raj, maintained their sentiments for the nation (Malik, 57-59).

The distinction Ch. Chhotu Ram drew between the rural-peasant Hindus and the urban-trading Hindus was broadly sensible. Whereas the former were largely drawn to communal formations, the latter saw their interests more in common with the Muslim and Sikh peasantry than with the urban Hindus. What Ch. Chhotu Ram wrote in *The Tribune* of 16 January 1926 clarifies this polarisation on both caste and economic lines.

The Unionist Party, he said, "seeks to unite Hindus, Mohammadans and Sikhs on the basis of their common secular and economic interests which are the only true foundations on which the edifice of lasting political parties can be raised. The party offers a common platform to all who desire to see the end of communal strife in the province. We are the friends of the poor, the supporters of the weak, helpers of the downtrodden, the advocates of the voiceless, and the champions of the exploited classes of the Punjab" (Datta, 120).

This has been the plank for the leaders from Ch. Chhotu Ram onwards, including Ch. Charan Singh and Ch. Devi Lal, to found new parties. If necessary, they would combine with a communal party to form a political alliance, but they would only use the alliance to protect their economic interests, and the moment the communal party went against these interests or pursued a purely communal agenda, they would part company with the political partner.

This broad alliance of farming communities, interestingly, allowed within its sphere one's stronger allegiance to one's caste. Ch. Chhotu Ram successfully played the peasant politics as well as the caste politics; the two worked like the smaller and the larger orbits around the same axis. Thus, with the Arya Samaj forming one commitment of the Jats and the land-proprietorship another, there obviously developed an ambivalence in their politics. They would be anti-Muslim if it came to cow protection, but they would be pro-Muslim if it came to protecting the land-owning interests. No wonder, the Non-Congress parties like the BKD, the BLD, the LD, the INLD, the RLD, all first formed and fostered by Ch. Charan Singh and Ch. Devi Lal and then continued and controlled by their sons, have been working with the love-hate relationship towards the Jan Singh and the BJP.

Gradually, the caste or community based parties in Haryana and Punjab have come to stay as regional powers, with the Congress Party as their permanent rival in the power politics. The uncomfortable alliance between the Zamindar or Jat Party, both in Haryana as well as Punjab, and the BJP is sustained, whenever it takes place, only by the sole necessity of keeping the Congress Party out of power. The ambiguities of the obscurantist politics represented by all these parties, including even the Congress, continues, keeping away the politics of ideology, which should remain above caste or community interests. No wonder, the idealogy-based parties like the CPI and the CPM have not been able to grow in this north-western region of India.

If one were to pinpoint the central driving force of Jat politics, one would find that it is the urge for dominance. The BJP, the Congress Party, or even the Communist Party, so long as it permits the Jats the dominant role, they would stay in the alliance. But the moment they are pushed into a subordinate position, they would part company. They would break the alliance; they would even break the party. Support from any party is welcome to them, so long as they can continue to rule. What they cannot brook for long is the position of subordination. Even in recent times, we know how the Jats in Rajasthan have been swinging between the Congress and the BJP – like one willing to woo but afraid to embrace. In U.P., the RLD of Ch. Ajit Singh has to search for a new ally in every election. By their smaller number in U.P., the Jats cannot hope to play the leading role. And yet, in U.P. Ch. Charan Singh broke parties and alliances only in search of dominance. Twice he succeeded, though for short periods of time. In fact, he succeeded even at the national level, becoming the Prime Minister of India for four months by breaking the Janata Party.

The Jat community's interests, as against those of the Mahajan and Brahman communities, were uppermost in Ch. Chhotu Ram's mind. To protect that citadel of his caste and its social and economic interests, he would not mind even siding with the British, whose interests he would indirectly be protecting. Since the Congress posed the main threat to the British interests in India, the anti-Congressism of Ch. Chotu Ram's Zamindar League suited them very well. In other words, driven by local politics of dominance, Ch. Chhotu Ram could remain indifferent to, and even go against, the national interests, serving indirectly the interests of British imperialism. Ch. Chhotu Ram's fear was that the Congress Party, allowing dominance to the superior or privileged castes over the peasant castes of the farming communities, would not help in his attempt to politically and economically strengthen these communities. He was keen to improve the lot of these tillers of the land at all costs. So he did, and quite successfully. Nationalism, he knew, would take care of itself.

This polarization between the Barahmans and Mahajans preferring the Congress and the Jats, Ahirs, etc., opting for the Zamindar League or the Unionist Party, gets reflected in a 1942-list of dangerous political agitators for whom history-sheets were maintained by the English Superintendent of Police at Rohtak. In this list, one finds that out of a total of 20 "dangerous agitators", whereas the Brahmans (4) and Mahajans (8) form the largest group, the Jats (6), Ahirs (1), Muslims (1) form a smaller group. Considered in relation to almost fifty percent population of the Jats in Rohtak district, the number in the list is small indeed.

The said list included Ch. Ranbir Singh Hooda as the only one from among the Jat leaders. The largest number of the

Mahajans may be owing to the influence of Lala Lajpat Rai and Mahatama Gandhi (who laid the foundation stone of Vaish High School, Rohtak, in the 1920's), whereas the smaller number of the numerically dominant caste of Jats could be because of their inclination towards the Unionist Party. In any case, the divide between the upper castes and the peasant castes clearly grouped them in the opposing camps of the Nationalists and the Unionists.

Thus, it was during the days of Ch. Chhotu Ram that the foundation was laid for the future politics, not only of Haryana but also of Punjab. It was he who had consolidated and sharpened the antagonism between the Jats and the non-Jats, the rural and the urban communities, the Congress and the non-Congress parties. These very antagonisms, we know, have continued to dominate the power politics both in modern Haryana as well as Punjab, right upto the bifurcation of the state of Punjab on November, 1966, as also thereafter.

On both sides, while the Congress has continued to be the major political force, the Akali Dal in Punjab and the Lok Dal in Haryana have to rely on the BJP's support for capturing power. The hunger for power has always brought together these strange bedfellows – the Akali Dal and the BJP in Punjab, and the Lok Dal and the BJP in Haryana. But for the common enemy (the Congress Party), neither the Akali Dal nor the Lok Dal would care to turn to the BJP, considered a party of those that exploit the peasants. As Ch. Devi Lal once remarked, the horse (the traders) and the fodder (the peasants) could not be companions.

The Land Alienation Act of 1900 was a decisive step that gave the Jats and the other castes attached to lands the property rights on their holdings, making them more assertive in social and political life. This Act, incidentally, prevented the transfer of agricultural land, by sale or otherwise, to non-agriculturists. Today, the situation is rather ironic, when the governments in different states, including West Bangal, where the ruling left parties have always claimed that their policies are pro-peasants, acquire agricultural land and sell it to the Corporate Sector for the purposes of industry and commerce. Of course, times have changed; even Ch. Chhotu Ram might have done the same as the present–day peasant leadership is doing. Globalization is posing hard choices, compelling the governments of the day, including the people's, to "liberalise" the economy; the choice is between development by capital investment, or development by the "poor" public sector. In our time, individuals are wealthier than the nations.

Whereas Ch. Chhotu Ram and other Zamindar leaders succeeded in liberating the Jats and other landed peasantry from the exploitation of the money-lenders, they also turned these land-owning peasants, at least the rich ones among them, into exploiters of the landless classes of the lower castes. This peasant dominance, in a way, continues in rural Haryana even today, although the times have greatly changed otherwise. We shall see later how political leaders from the lower castes still remain secondary members of the ruling outfit, whichever party may have formed the government. Just as in business today the rich are getting richer and the poor poorer, so in politics, the strong are getting stronger, the weak weaker.

In this formative period of Haryana politics, we can see how antagonisms were born and consolidated, leading to political rivalries between the urban and the rural, the traders and the peasants, the land-owning and the landless. Above all, the seminal formations in the power politics of the Haryana region gave an early lead to the districts of Rohtak and Hissar. Largely because of Ch. Chhotu Ram's leadership, but also because of the caste-based efforts of certain other leaders of that community, these two districts with Jat majority achieved supremacy in the power politics of Haryana, which supremacy continues even today. Even the change of government from the imperial to the national has not made any difference in the caste and class structures of our society. Those leading in the colonial regime are also the leading ones today, in politics as well as business, in caste leadership as well as caste dominance, in urban prosperity as well as rural poverty.

Also, the national Congress versus the regional forces based on the Jat-led agriculture communities, and the religion based BJP, remains a major political antagonism even today. It is with these crosscurrents of political creeds and crusades, aversions and antagonisms, that the politics of Haryana has developed over the years, seldom making any major departure from the foundations laid in the decades preceding our independence in 1947. Nor did the antagonism and the power structure change much even after the formation of the new state of Haryana in 1966, except that in the narrower arena of the state's power politics those antagonisms have acquired a sharper edge.

Within the Congress Party also, both in Punjab and Haryana, right from the days of Sardar Partap Singh Kairon and Professor Sher Singh down to the present time of Sardar Amrinder Singh and Ch. Bhupinder Singh Hooda, the Jats have continuously pressed their claim to dominance; whenever that dominance has not been permitted, by whatever combination of forces, both the states have witnessed turmoils, toppling the governments, at times even at the cost of the party. The internal struggles within the Congress have been a reflection of the external struggles between the Congress and the opposition, the battle-lines remaining just about the same in both the states. In other words, the power politics in Haryana, as well as in Punjab before its bifurcation in 1966, has been dominated by the Jats. We shall see how this caste factor, a gift of Ch. Chhotu Ram for the most part, has continued to determine the course of power politics in the region (later made a state) of Haryana. Whether we like it or not, the dominance of the major caste or community in each state of the Indian Union is a hard fact; it is inbuilt into the fabric of our democracy, and cannot be wished away so long as the present form of our political ideology continues.

2

The Post-Chhotu Ram Period 1945-1957

When Ch. Chhotu Ram died in 1945, the mantle of leadership of the Zamindar League fell on Ch. Tika Ram of Sonepat, who succeeded as Minister his mentor in the Government of the Unionist Party in Punjab. He was made of a slightly different metal, lacking the passion and dynamism of Ch. Chhotu Ram, who had succeeded in the gigantic task of establishing political dominance of the Jats in the province of Punjab, especially in the region now named Haryana. Ch. Tika Ram did not have the political acumen of Ch. Chhotu Ram, more interested as he was in the educational field and social service than in organizing the peasant politics. He became the founder of Chhotu Ram Zamindar High School and Chhotu Ram Arya College at Sonepat, to which task he devoted himself after losing the Aseembly election from Sonepat constituency to Ch. Lehri Singh in 1946.

Meanwhile, a new crop of Jat leadership had emerged in Rohtak, Hisar and Karnal districts. In the Sonepat Tehsil of

Rohtak district alone there came up stalwarts like Ch. Lehri Singh and Ch. Mukhtiar Singh, both from the same village located near the city of Sonepat; Pandit Chiranji Lal and Ch. Rizak Ram, both settled in the city of Sonepat; all of whom came into prominence around the same time. These leaders, like their predecessors - Ch. Lal Chand and Ch. Chhotu Ram, etc. — were lawyers by profession. In the district of Hisar emerged leaders like Ch. Suraj Mal and Captain Ranjit Singh.

More important than any of these leaders emerged from a border village of Haryana, Chautala, the two brothers, namely, Ch. Sahib Ram and Ch. Devi Lal. This Chautala family had its initial association with the Congress Party; Ch. Devi Lal took active part in the Freedom Movement. Although Ch. Ranbir Singh Hooda, son of Ch. Matu Ram of Sanghi village, had a longer period of participation in the Freedom Movement than did Ch. Devi Lal, the latter was more quick in seizing initiatives for leading local agitations. Along with Pandit Sri Ram Sharma, Ch. Ranbir Singh had been to jail several times in the 1940's and had successfully contested election to the National Constituent Assembly. It is a matter of pride for this leading Hooda family of Sanghi today that while Ch. Rambir Singh is the only surviving member of that Assembly, responsible for the drafting of the Constitution of India, his son, Ch. Bhupinder Singh Hooda, is the Chief Minister of Haryana.

In the 1946 - election of the Punjab Assembly, the Zamindar League had to face defeat in all the three seats of Rothak, namely Jhajjar, Rohtak, and Sonepat, from where respectively the three Congress leaders elected were Professor Sher Singh, Ch. Badlu Ram and Ch. Lehri Singh. Incidentally, Ch. Badlu Ram also belonged to the village Sanghi, made famous by the Hooda family. Regional and local parties, it may be noted here, generally decline and disappear with the demise of their founder leaders, unless the leaders have after them able heirs in the family to continue the political agenda. The demise of the Zamindar League was quite natural after the death of Ch. Chhotu Ram.

The rural rowdyism of the Zamindar League was once again demonstrated in this election, more glaringly so at the election meetings organised in the constituency of Jhajjar, which were addressed by Pandit Jawaharlal Nehru and the elder brother of Subhas Chander Bose. As ususal, the rowdyism reflected frustration – an indication that the party that once ruled the region was now on the way out. The Zamindar League lost the election. The Congress Party formed the government, though with the help of regional parties, (interestingly) including the Zamindar Party. It needs to be noted here that though the Congress Party had the largest number of seats, the Chief Minister became Khizar Hyat Khan of the Zamindar Party. The Government of Khan had a total of six Ministers with three Hindus and three Muslims. Decidedly, the British had successfully effected and consolidated the communal divide in Punjab. Shri Bhim Sen Sachar of the Congress Party was elected leader and became a Minister in the Coalition Government comprising the Congress Party, the Zamindar League, and the Akali Dal. From the Congress side, besides Sh. Sachar, Ch. Lehri Singh also became a minister. The latter represented the Haryana region.

Since Ch. Chhotu Ram had no son, his nephew, Ch. Shri Chand, became his successor at Rohtak. Also, the husband of Ch. Chhotu Ram's daughter, Ch. Neki Ram, got prominence in the Jind area. Neither of them, however, could reach anywhere near the fame Ch. Chhotu Ram enjoyed, although both had the advantage of having been his close relations. Both Ch. Shri Chand and Ch. Neki Ram did become legislators once or twice, but their politics did not go a long way. Ch. Shri Chand did become the Speaker of the Haryana Assembly in 1967, but only for a few months and thereafter disappeared from the scene. Ch. Neki Ram was ably succeeded by his son, Ch. Birender Singh, who is still in active politics and has been in the front-rank politics of the Haryana Congress Party since 1977.

From 1945 to the creation of Haryana in 1966, the role of the legislators from the Hayrana region was only to act as a pressure group to counter the Akali Dal, which was all the time pressing for a separate Punjabi Suba. While the Akali Dal kept pressing for the claim of the Punjabi language as the sole official language of the new state of Punjab, after the partition of 1947, the seat of power (the chief ministership) continued to witness the see-saw battle between Shri Bhim Sen Sachar and Dr. Gopi Chand Bhargav. These two Congress leaders had well-formed groups with patronage from two powerful central leaders. Since the Congress did not have a clear majority in the state Assembly, neither in 1946 nor in 1952, it was dependent on the Akali Dal and the Muslim League — more on the Akali Dal.

The Akali Dal's politics was to back whoever agreed to favour the Punjabi language as the official language of the state. The Hindu Mahasabha of Punjab and the Arya Samaj of Haryana region wanted safeguards for the Hindi-speaking people of Punjab. Thus came up a division among the legislators and their political parties based on communal affiliations; the Hindus and the Sikhs, united before the partition of 1947, united against the Muslims (except, of course, those in the Unionist Party), but now forming two separate religious and political camps.

While the shifting Akali support from one to the other prospective Chief Minister made the seat of power a musical-chair race between Sh. Sachar and Dr. Bhargav, the Punjabi-speaking Hindus took contradictory stands in the two regions; in favour of Hindi in the Punjab region, and in favour of Punjabi in the Haryana region. The fear among the Hindus of Punjab was that the state may be split, creating two smaller states on a linguistic basis as was being done all over the country. In that case, the Punjabi-speaking Hindus on both sides would lose their political dominance or advantage and would be dominated instead by the Jats in the 'new' states. Their fears were not unfounded. Quite often, the Akalis (the Sikh Jats by and large) and the Jat legislators from the Haryana region combined to force things their way, wherever their common rural or peasant interests were involved. The Punjabi-speaking Hindus knew the Jats well enough to be wary of their certain dominance, if the state was to be divided on a linguistic basis. Hence their contradictory stands in the two parts of the same state.

As a safeguard for their own interests, the Punjabi-speaking Hindus raised the slogan of Maha Punjab, which was meant to include some areas from Rajasthan and U.P. as well. As a counter move to this, the Jats and their allies in the Haryana region raised the slogan of Vishal Haryana or Maha Dilli, which desired to include, besides the Ambala Division of Punjab (Haryana region), Delhi, western U.P., and parts of Rajasthan.

The Union Government could not favour either of the two proposals because neither was consistent with its policy of linguistic states for which a Commission had been appointed at the national level. In view of the terms of reference given to the Commission, the two proposals sounded rather preposterous, inspired as they were by interests other than those related to language and culture. The interests on both sides were purely political. The question was of political dominance, not of linguistic and cultural cohesion.

The three power groups – the Akalis, the Haryana Jats, the Punjabi-speaking Hindus – wanted each a state of their own choice so that the political playground became favourable for the group's dominance. Finally, as could be expected, the Akalis won the race, and so did the Jats of Haryana, both securing a state each for their dominance. No wonder, after the formation of the states of the present Punjab and Haryana, there has been no Punjabi-speaking Hindu Chief-Minister on either side. Realising the force of majoritarianism in the Indian democracy, so loudly depicted in the two states, this community has abandoned their political ambition and concentrated instead on private business and professional services.

Going back to the post-Chhotu Ram and post-Independence politics in the region now named Haryana, the new stars that dominated these years were Professor Sher Singh and Ch. Devi Lal, although stalwarts like Ch. Lehri Singh, Pandit Sri Ram Sharma, Ch. Suraj Mal were still active in the political arena. The duo of Prof. Sher Singh and Ch. Devi Lal spearheaded the politics of the region during the years 1946-66, fighting for the regional interests, sacrificing their personal ones, whenever the occasion so demanded.

An M.A. in Mathematics from the University of Delhi, Professor Sher Singh had taught for some years at the All India Jat Heroes Memorial College at Rohtak before he contested the Punjab Assembly election in 1946. Ch. Devi Lal had joined political activism right after his school education, fighting for the cause of the peasantry in Punjab, later taking an active part in the Freedom Movement. The two together took up the cause of Haryana and pursued it relentlessly.

A close associate of the two leaders was Ch. Badlu Ram of Sanghi village who had also been elected to the Punjab Assembly in 1946. The trio emerged as the Jat-Arya Samaj lobby from the Haryana region. While Professor Sher Singh was more committed to the Arya Samaj movement, Ch. Devi Lal had greater commitment to the farming community, his politics being similar to that of Ch. Chhotu Ram. Ch. Badlu Ram, a Jat by caste, personally loyal to Professor Sher Singh, remained equally committed to the Arya Samaj as well as to the Jat community of the Haryana region.

Ch. Ranbir Singh Hooda was equally committed to the Arya Samaj and to the Congress Swatantra Party. Unlike Professor Sher Singh and Ch. Devi Lal, and before them Ch. Chhotu Ram, he would not quit the party for any regional or casteist cause. He has remained a true servant of the Congress Party, very much a man of John Milton's description: "They also serve who only stand and wait." The three generations of this Hooda family of Sanghi have been in the Congress Party as also in the Arya Samaj, but none of the family ever deviated from their firm commitment to the Congress Party. They kept their personal ambitions at bay whenever it came to showing loyalty to their political party. In that respect, this family has been unlike the other families of Jat leaders, whereas others left the party whenever it came to fighting for the peasantry (primarily Jats) or for personal ambition. Of course, the patient servingmen may not attain the glory of those that rebel against the ruling power, and may remain lusterless, they do get rewarded at long last for their loyalty to the party. Maintaining their loyalty to the Congress Party, the Hoodas did receive their rewards. While Ch. Ranbir Singh remained one of the leading political figures in the state for four decades, becoming more than once a Minister in the state government and a Member of Parliament at the centre, his son Ch. Bhupinder Singh Hooda is now the Chief Minister of Haryana, while the family has its fourth generation Dipender Hooda as an M.P. from Rohtak.

Thus, while Prof. Sher Singh and Ch. Devi Lal remained rebels all through their political careers, fighting for causes dear to them, Ch. Ranbir Singh Hooda, carrying the family tradition of total loyalty, remained a staunch party worker. He did get his reward in his long political career, but never attained the halo of a popular hero. He remained a quiet performer all his life. If the duo of the rebels got the hero's reception at times, they also remained at the receiving end at other times.

The families of Ch. Lal Chand and Seth Chhaju Ram, two other prominent leaders of the Chhotu Ram era, after their early participation in the Jat and the Arya Samaj politics, had settled in business, both becoming creators of the leading business—houses one time or another. Ch. Lal Chand got a bad name by getting too close to the British rulers, so much so that he was alleged to have appeared as a witness in favour of General Dyer, notorious for the massacre of Jhalianwala Bagh. His legacy is the DLF business house, a muti-national company at present, having nothing much to do with the state of Haryana as such. Seth Chhaju Ram was not much interested in politics right from the beginning. Only once he contested election to the Punjab Council as an independent candidate in 1926 and got elected, defeating one Rai Sahib Lajpat Rai of village Sisai. He did remain active in the leadership role of the Jat community, helped Ch. Chhotu Ram financially, and even got built the famous

Chhotu Ram Kothi at Rohtak. Pandit Sri Ram Sharma, a rival to Ch. Chhotu Ram, who faded out in politics after Independence, was succeeded in the caste politics by Pandit Bhagwat Dayal Sharma who came into prominence, along with Ch. Bansi Lal, in the early 1960's.

In the district of Hisar, besides the duo of Ch. Devi Lal and his elder brother Ch. Sahib Ram, there emerged in the 1940's leaders like Captain Ranjit Singh and Ch. Suraj Mal. In 1947, Ch. Lehri Singh from Rohtak district and Captain Ranjit Singh from Hisar were made Ministers in the Cabinet headed by Dr. Gopi Chand Bhargav. As it seems, the initiative for dominance in the ministerial politics, as well as in making assertions of power for the Haryana region against the dominance of the region of Punjab, remained with the Jats.

While during the days of Ch. Chhotu Ram, the centre of power for the region was Rohtak, after Ch. Chhotu Ram, it came to be shared between Rohtak and Hisar districts, both comprising the areas dominated by the Jat community. These two districts now stand divided into seven smaller districts. Certain individuals like Pandit Sri Ram Sharma, Ch. Chand Ram (an S.C.) did enjoy importance as Ministers or leaders of their respective communities, but they could not raise a force behind them to represent the region or challenge the elder brother, the Punjabi region.

Professor Sher Singh attained more eminence when, soon after Independence, the district of Rothak was chosen for prohibition. As a staunch Arya Samaji, it was an issue dear to his heart. He took the lead and made it a movement to commit people to observing prohibition voluntarily, without inviting enforcement by the iron hand of the law. This measure brought Professor Sher Singh closer to Mahatma Gandhi; no other Haryana leader got such an opportunity. It needs to be noted that most Haryana leaders from Ch. Chhotu Ram to Professor Sher Singh had become staunch followers of the Arya Samaj during their student days at the University of Delhi, which was both a reformist as well as a nationist movement, inculcating in the youth a reverence for their own heritage.

Around the same time, in 1948, social boycott of the Scheduled Castes was declared by the Jats of Bhaproda village in Rohtak district. The cause of this social boycott was a minor incident between two families belonging to the two castes. Here, again, Prof. Sher Singh, accompanied by Ch. Badlu Ram, his Hanuman, resolved the dispute by impressing upon the various castes that if they promised peace in the village, a public meeting would be organized in that village which would be addressed by Mahatma Gandhi. The villagers felt elated and agreed to Prof. Sher Singh's mediation and suggestion. The dispute was thus resolved amicably (Singh, 47).

Between 1946 and 1955, the ding-dong battle for the post of the Chief Minister of Punjab between Sh. Bhim Sen Sachar and Dr. Gopi Chand Bhargav continued, each removed more than once by the other through a motion of no-confidence. The power-table in respect of the Chief Ministership of Punjab emerges as under:

1946	:	Shri Bhim Sen Sachar
1947	:	Dr Gopi Chand Bahrgav
1949	:	Shri Bhim Sen Sachar
1949	:	Dr. Gopi Chand Bhargav
1952	:	Shri Bhim Sen Sachar

The Government of Punjab got stability only when Sardar Partap Singh Kairon replaced Sh. Bhim Sen Sachar in January 1956, one year before the election due next year. By this time, the pressure tactics of the Akalis for the creation of a Punjabi Suba had started working. The behind-the-scene agreement between the Akalis and the legislators of Ambala Division (now Haryana), most of whom were Jats, was that after Shri Sachar's removal, Sardar Partap Singh Kairon would be the Chief Minister, with someone from the Haryana region as the Deputy Chief Minister. The Haryana pressure-group that lobbied for this formula included Ch. Devi Lal, Professor Sher Singh, Babu Mool Chand Jain of Karnal, Ch. Badlu Ram and five others. They succeeded in getting Prof. Sher Singh appointed to the post of Deputy Chief Minister.

These two lobbies, though wedded to different regional interests, had two things in common: one, both favoured the Jat dominance in the government of Punjab; two, both wanted the division of Punjab to the advantage of the Jat community, to which both the lobbies largely belonged. The strategy worked, and ultimately the parallel moves of Maha Punjab and Maha Delhi or Vishal Haryana failed. In fact, these proposals were never meant to succeed; they were raised only to defeat each other. The real demands were for a Punjabi Suba with the dominance of the Sikh Jats, and for a Haryana Pradesh with the dominance of the Hindu Jats. Both ultimately got what they wanted, though after a long struggle for more than fifteen years, which went through various stages from the formation of the Sachar Language Formula to the appointment of the Boundary Commission.

The creation of Haryana was not just a byproduct of the Akali agitation's success in securing a Punjabi-speaking state, a parallel move, albeit less powerful than that of the Akalis, was always afoot in the Hindi-speaking region, mostly headed by Prof. Sher Singh and Ch. Devi Lal. For instance, Prof. Sher Singh had launched the *Hindi Satyagrah* in 1957 to protect the interests of the Hindi-speaking population of Punjab (now Haryana). He had resigned his job in the Cabinet, in which he was Deputy Chief Minister, as also from the Congress Party, and made the *Satyagrah* a mass movement in which thousands of people went to jail.

Ch. Devi Lal had just been released from the Ferozpore jail where he had been sent as a leader-protestor against the tillers' dispossession of their lands. Although after the Assembly election of 1957, when S. Partap Singh Kairon took over again as the Congress Chief Minister, the Zamindar Party, a legacy of Ch. Chhotu Ram, was in a way liquidated, as all its leaders including Ch. Shri Chand, Ch. Maru Singh, etc., joined the Congress Party, thereby making the Jat force a formidable pressure-group within the Congress Party. While Ch. Devi Lal was almost the lone fighter from the Hisar district, others being not so active in power politics, caring more for their personal interests, the Rohtak district, Prof. Sher Singh was able to gather around him several prominent Jat leaders. The Arya Samaj, not the Jat community, being the principal commitment of Professor Sher Singh, his following included masses from other castes as well. Ch. Devi Lal had greater appeal in his own community of the Jats.

A one-time miracle happened for the Communist Party of India – the only Communist Party at the time – when in the 1957-election its candidate from Rohtak Parliamentary Constituency, Ch. Partap Singh Daulta, won the contest. Two Assembly seats were also won by the CPI with Ch. Hukam Singh

Dahiya securing the Sampla seat and Sh. Phool Singh Kataria that of Jhajjar. Both defeated important leaders of the area, respectively Ch. Lehri Singh and Ch. Chand Ram. It was also because of the great influence of Ch. Devi Lal and Prof. Sher Singh on the voters of the Jat community that these stalwarts lost the elections. Ch. Chand Ram had grown ambitious and was trying to defeat Prof. Sher Singh, hoping to get an important position in the Cabinet. But he was not fully aware of the powerful influence Prof. Sher Singh enjoyed among the Jat voters, who were the deciding factor in Rohtak and Hisar districts.

Here, we also need to note that in the power politics of Haryana, defeating your rivals within your own party is more important for the political leaders than securing a majority for their party. Each leader, therefore, with some political ambition, even that of going ahead of the rivals at the district level, would work for the defeat of his own party candidates in that district. When the stakes are higher, investments of money and muscle power, of caste and community sentiments, are also made in equal measure. The fact that even a person like Professor Sher Singh, considered highly cultured among the Haryana politicians of his time, could take to these tactics of undercutting the rivals in his own party proves the compulsive nature of the instinct for survival. No wonder the Darwinian principles of "struggle for existence" and "survival of the fittest" are as valid in politics as they are in the animal world.

It also needs to be noted that caste imparts a strong affinity among its members across all boundaries—religious, regional, provincial, professional, or whatever. We have seen how the Akalis of Punjab and the Arya Samajis of Haryana felt close to each other because of the common caste factor. We have also seen how the Jat leaders in Ch. Chhotu Ram's time worked in tandem across political lines whenever any matter concerning the community was involved. Caste ties in India, it seems, have remained quite strong through centuries, overriding even ethical or moral considerations. The fact that caste leaders enjoy a large following today – even those with shady moral status – shows how strong Manu's system has been in the structure and growth of Indian societies.

3

Towards The Creation of Haryana 1957-1967

After the Hindi Andolan – a combined assertion of the Hindus from both regions (North and South) of the state against the imposition of Punjabi as a compulsory language for all in Punjab – another important instance of the assertion of identity by the people of the southern region of Punjab was the Parliamentary by–election of the Gurgaon Constituency in 1958. In 1957, Maulana Abul Kalam Azad had been elected from this constituency, but his death necessitated the by–election the next year. The Congress Party's High Command nominated Pandit Mauli Chand Sharma who had just joined the party after quitting the Jan Sangh. Professor Sher Singh and his colleagues from the Arya Samaj and the Hindi lobby put up Shri Prakash Vir Shastri, a staunch Arya Samaji, as an independent candidate. The defeat of the Congress candidate in this election was significant in that it implied a warning from the emerging power of the Arya Samaj and the Jat peasantry, clearly heading towards demarcating a political territory of their own in which they would call the shots.

The next stage of the regional assertion for a separate identity of the Hindi-speaking southern region of Punjab (now Haryana) is represented by the movement launched for the creation of Vishal Haryana around the same time (1958). The leader of this movement, too, was Professor Sher Singh. Between the death of Ch. Chhotu Ram in 1945 and the creation of Haryana in 1966, Professor Sher Singh remained the undisputed representative voice of the people of Haryana. He not only articulated the interests of the people of the region but provided unblemished leadership to the neglected populace of southern Punjab. People followed him, responding to his call for whatever form of struggle he proposed for securing a rightful place to the people of the southern region of Punjab, dominated and degraded by the Punjabi-speaking northern region. Professor Sher Singh not only succeeded in getting his voice heard, he also got recognition to the region he represented as an independent linguistic and cultural unit of the country having legitimate claims of its own.

The movement for Vishal Haryana may not have met with much success, but the idea of a separate state for the people of the southern region of Punjab, having a distinct language and culture of their own, certainly got registered in the minds of the majority of those involved in the various crusades Professor Sher Singh had launched in the last fifteen years or so. This was not a small success for an individual leader. In his various movements for the different causes of the people of the region now called Haryana, this soft but stubborn leader had several allies, including Ch. Devi Lal, Babu Mool Chand Jain, and Pandit Sri Ram Sharma. Between the Partition of 1947 and the Assembly election of 1957, whereafter he got his political position as Deputy Chief Minister of Punjab, Professor Sher Singh had not only attained the stature of a leader but also gathered a sizeable following of even non-Jat supporters. This support extended far beyond his native land (now called Haryana); he gained popularity among the Hindus of Punjab as also among the people of U.P. and Rajasthan living in the districts bordering Haryana. After Ch. Chhotu Ram he was the only Jat leader at that time to have gained such a wide area of influence. Later, Ch. Charan Singh and Ch. Devi Lal rose to enjoy a similar status in Haryana, Rajasthan and U.P.

Meanwhile, the Akalis in Punjab had intensified their efforts for the creation of a separate Punjabi Suba. Unable to ignore or repress the Akali Movement, the Union Government headed by Pandit Jawahalal Nehru appointed in 1961 Justice A.R. Das, a judge of the Supreme Court of India, to look into the alleged regional imbalance in respect of recruitments in the government departments and the Public Undertakings. Better known as the 'Das Commission', its appointment was the result of increasing representations from both sides of the linguistic divide between the northern and the southern parts of Punjab, the two sides being headed respectively by the Akali Dal in the North and the Haryana Lok Samiti in the South. While the Akali Dal worked under the leadership of Master Tara Singh, the Haryana Lok Samiti functioned under the leadership of Professor Sher Singh.

If the Akalis were superior in having a large following of committed cadres, the Samiti had an advantage in Professor Sher Singh's ability to articulate Haryana's interests wholly based on facts and figures. The latter's learning in Mathmatics, his staunch sincerity to the Arya Samaj, and his sense of responsibility towards his region was unmatched at the time. His followers were there to respond to any call he made for an agitation. His hard work showed results; the Das Commission upheld his contention that although the protests were louder from the Akali side, injustice was actually being continued against the people of the Hindi-speaking region. Professor Sher Singh thus scored a victory of sorts. Meanwhile, the Assembly election of 1962 was nearing, which gave this learned leader of the Haryana region a new task to perform.

S. Partap Singh Kairon as Chief Minister of Punjab was determined to finish off the leadership of both the Akali Dal and the Haryana Lok Samiti so that he could rule the state with no opposition to his autocracy. To achieve his goal in the Haryana region, he put up Pandit Bhagwat Dayal Sharma, a green horn in politics, associated with the labour wing of the Congress Party, against Professor Sher Singh from the Jhajjar constituency. The earlier antagonism between the Congress Party headed by Pandit Sri Ram Sharma and the Zamindar League headed by Ch. Chhotu Ram was replayed.

The Congress Party went all out to change the entire complexion of the election into the dynamics of the old caste-based politics. The atmosphere in the villages got vitiated once more. The polarisation took place on the lines of the Jats versus the others. Besides, Sardar Partap Singh Kairon used all means of money and muscle power, official machinery as well as private machinations, to ensure the defeat of Professor Sher Singh.

The election result went in favour of the Congress candidate, though not without allegations of manipulation in counting. Professor Sher Singh was declared to have lost by a margin of 1000 votes. People were not ready to accept the verdict. They descended from all sides on the venue of counting at Jhajjar, forming a huge crowd of threatening proportions. In keeping with his high character, inspired by tall ideals, the leader adopted the peaceful course. Although he had to dole out a few innocent lies to his followers, he was able to diffuse the volatile situation. The leader may have lost, but the Samiti managed to win six Assembly seats and the prestigious Rohtak Lok Sabha seat.

Here, an intresting anecdote comes to mind. Along with Professor Sher Singh, Ch. Partap Singh Daulta of the Congress Party had lost in the 1962 election to the Parliament from the Rohtak constituency. Known for his foul tongue, Sh. Daulta lost, as his friends and followers pointed out to him, because of his impolite language. When Sh. Daulta heard this, his prompt reply was, "How about Professor Sher Singh, the apostle of politeness, who would offer salutations even to electric poles? Why did he lose?" Ch. Daulta's argument was irrefutable. And he was quite right. Political victories or defeats are not caused by polite or pernicious dictions; in these matters, reasons are political, not cultural.

The Haryana leader's defeat, however, proved a blessing in disguise; Professor Sher Singh was now free to devote his whole time to preparing the case for the creation of a separate state for the people of the Hindi-speaking region of Punjab. In fact, he could now adopt a more militant posture than would have been possible while remaining a member of the legislature; his posture now matched that of the Akalis. His defeat, the way it was ensured, gave his mission a greater punch, and he worked day and night to make his crusade a success. The political advantage of Professor Sher Singh's agitations for the Hindi language and the Haryana region was not limited to his Haryana Lok Samiti alone; the Haryanvis of all hues who had joined the Hindi Andolan in the late 1950's gained prominence in public as brave sons of the soil, and as protectors of the mother tongue.

In the Punjab Assembly election of 1962, even the Jan Sangh (not a major political force in the Haryana region those days) reaped the fruits of its support to the Hindi Andolan. Besides winning several seats in the state Assembly, the Jan Sangh won three seats in the Parliament election held the same year. From the three Jat-dominated districts of Rohtak, Hisar, and Karnal, Ch. Lehri Singh, Ch. Yudhvir Singh, and Swami Rameshwaranand respectively got elected defeating their Congress rivals. After the creation of Haryana, this party now called the BJP has never had it so good.

For the consolidation of the non-Congress forces in the region of Haryana, the twin elections of 1962 proved quite crucial. Besides the emergence of the Haryana Lok Samiti and the Jan Sangh as formidable poltical forces, Ch. Devi Lal in the Hisar district got elected independently, since he had been denied the Congress ticket that year. The reason for the denial was the dominant influence of Sardar Partap Singh Kairon, who, after becoming the Chief Minister with the help of Prof. Sher Singh and Ch. Devi Lal, besides others of their group from the Hindi-speaking region of Punjab, had turned hostile towards his makers. The fact that 23 seats out of a total of 54 in the Haryana region went to the non-Congress candidates is evidence to the consolidation of the opposition groups. It was for the first time after Independence that the Congress Party felt challenged by the "other" political parties in the state. Earlier, there was hardly any challenge, not at least of this magnitude.

A true ally as Ch. Devi Lal always remained in politics, never deceiving his friends, he felt concerned about the defeat of Professor Sher Singh. The two had worked as comrades in several movements for protecting the rights of the people of the region now called Haryana. He mustered support for

Professor Sher Singh from the non-Congress legistators and got him elected to the State Council, making him an MLC, if not an MLA. This event made it possible once again for the regional leaders to combine and collect their might for a decisive battle for protecting the interests of their people against the aggressive onslaught of the Akalis and others working for a seprate Punjabi Suba.

Finding the Punjab problem running into dire straits, the Prime Minister of India, Smt. Indira Gandhi, appointed, after the 1965 war with Pakistan, a Committee of Parliament headed by the Speaker, Sardar Hukam Singh, with Ch. Lehri Singh and Ch. Bansi Lal (a member of the Rajya Sabha elected in 1962) as members to represent the Haryana region. The election of Ch. Bansi Lal to the Rajya Sabha, incidentally, involves an interesting incident, not out of place to narrate in the present context.

Sh. Dhebar Bhai, the then President of the Congress Party, had been briefed by interested elements that no Jat should be nominated to the Rajya Sabha, as they were already in dominant position both in the Lok Sabha as well as the State Assembly. Ch. Devi Lal, being the regional leader in the party, pleaded for one name after another, all from the Jat community, but Dhebar Bhai rejected all, saying no Jat was acceptable to him. Using his ready wit Ch. Devi Lal said, then in that case Shri Bansi Lal ji could be the party's nominee, concealing, that, he, too, was from the Jat community. Seeing no "Singh" in the name, Dhebar Bhai thought the person must be a non-Jat, perhaps a Bania. That is how, Ch. Devi Lal himself once told the author, Ch. Bansi Lal was smuggled into the Rajya Sabha.

Returning to the Hukam Singh Committee of Parliament appointed to find a solution to the increasing Punjab problem, we must note that while Ch. Bansi Lal expressed his opinion against the creation of a small state like Haryana, Ch. Lehri Singh lent all his weight in favour of it. Ch. Lehri Singh's stand was not liked by the Jan Sangh Party of which he was a member. The Jan Singh in Punjab was largely the party of the Punjabi Hindus, especially those who migrated from the region that became a part of Paskitan, and was demanding the Maha Punjab so that the Sikhs remained a minority community in the state. When the party conveyed its displeasure to Ch. Lehri Singh, he smartly said, "Well, I might have contested on your symbol of Diva (earthen lamp), but the wick and oil in it was mine own." In other words, his contention was that whereas the party symbol was only nominal, it was his personal following that won him the election. So, on the issue of Haryana, he resigned from the party, refusing to sacrifice the cause of the people of Haryana.

While the Jat leaders in the Congress Party, such as Ch. Ranbir Singh, even while remaining bound by the party discipline, supported the cause of the people of Haryana, others like Ch. Sultan Singh, Ch. Randhir Singh, Ch. Hardwari Lal and Rao Birender Singh actively opposed the cause and played the game Sardar Partap Singh Kairon wanted them to play. The reason why these leaders chose to side with the Chief Minister, who was openly opposed to the bifurcation of Punjab, was their own rivalry with the duo of Professor Sher Singh and Ch. Devi Lal. As the tussel between the forces in favour of the bifurcation of Punjab and those opposed to it took a serious turn, Ch. Devi Lal joined the Haryana Lok Samiti, becoming one of its leading lights. A test of loyalties came when in late 1965 the Haryana Lok Samiti decided to make a show of strength by organizing a public rally at Rohtak.

Whereas Professor Sher Singh and Ch. Devi Lal, under the banner of the Haryana Lok Samiti, had invited Shri Acharya Kriplani as the chief guest, a counter rally to defeat the former was organized in the same town by the Congress leaders including Pandit Bhagwat Dayal Sharma, Ch. Randhir Singh, Ch. Sultan Singh, Ch. Hardwari Lal, Rao Birender Singh, etc., with the Vice President of India, Dr. Zakir Hussain, as chief guest. While the Samiti leaders were mobilizing people for a call to create a separate state of Haryana, the Congress leaders were out to defeat the move.

The masses were found in overwhelming numbers on the side of the Samiti, and a very small number could be managed to counter the popular move. Ch. Hardwari Lal organized another rally in his own village, inviting Sardar Darbara Singh as the chief guest, which was attended by the same Congress leaders present at the Rohtak rally. Even this rally could not match the one organized by the pro–Haryana leaders – Professor Sher Singh and Ch. Devi Lal.

The Akalis were asking for a Punjabi Suba, but they were against the creation of Haryana. Their clever move was to separate from Punjab only the districts of Rohtak, Gurgoan, and Mahendergarh, where Sikhs had no presence, and merge them with U.P. or Rajasthan, converting the rest of Punjab into Punjabi Suba. But with the intensive efforts of Professor Sher Singh, Ch. Devi Lal and other leaders from the Haryana region, Sant Fateh Singh, by now the head of the Akalis, agreed that the representatives of the two warring regions, or factions, should sit together and solve the problem between themselves. From the Haryana side, Ch. Ranbir Singh, Ch. Devi Lal, Babu Anad Swaroop, Lala Ram Sharan Chand Mittal, besides the President of the All Party Action Committee, Professor Sher

Singh, joined the crucial meeting. It was jointly decided that the Regional Formula of 1956 be made the basis for the division of Punjab into two states to be called Punjab and Haryana (Singh, 101; the narration of most events in the foregoing pages of this chapter is based on Dr Ranjit Singh's book.).

Working on the agreed formula, the Shah Commission, appointed for the purpose, completed the job. But soon came a call from the Akalis that the award of the city of Chandigarh to Haryana was not acceptable to them, leading to a protracted agitation with both sides pressing their claims with an individual on either side sitting on 'fast-unto-death'. Leaving untold the long story of Chandigarh, which still remains a disputed territory, it is enough to say that the two states were finally created on November I, 1966. While the bifurcation of Punjab boosted the prospects of the Akalis in Punjab and the Samiti leaders in Haryana, those opposed to the idea on both sides received a set back.

Before the election could be organized, an interim government was appointed on either side. On the Haryana side, with the sixty two legislators, out of which the Congress Party had just a little over half the mark, Pandit Bhagwat Dayal Sharma was made the Chief Minister of Haryana, although there were several leaders in the same party far senior to him. Professor Sher Singh, Ch. Devi Lal and Ch. Lehri Singh, being in the opposition, were naturally not in the race for the Chief Ministership. But Ch. Ranbir Singh, Rao Birender Singh, Ch. Hardwari Lal, Ch. Suiraj Mal, etc., were in the Congress Party, all senior to Pandit Bhagwat Dayal Sharma.

The selection of Pandit Bhagwat Dayal Sharma as the Chief Minister of the new state of Haryana made the other leaders, the Jats in particular, sore; they felt convinced that the Congress Party was, after all, meant to serve the interests of the non-farming communities. The choice spited other farming communities as well. Rao Birender Singh, who had been a Minister in Punjab, was especially sore over the decision. All in all, this unfortunate choice of a dark horse to head the government of the new state (for no one knew him in politics before 1962 when he was picked up by Sardar Partap Singh Kairon, the then Chief Minister of Punjab, to defeat Professor Sher Singh by means fair and foul) revivied the Jat-Brahman antagonism earlier symbolized by the rivalry of Ch. Chhotu Ram and Pandit Sri Ram Sharma. The power politics of Haryana thus went back to its original form shaped by Ch. Chhotu Ram, who had consolidated the Jats and other peasant communities against the Brahman-Bania dominated Congress Party.

This event of 1966 sharpened the old suspicion of the Jats, their suspicion of the Congress being an anti-Jat party, a party of the Brahman-Baniya combine. This antagonism had both a cultural as well as an economic basis: while culturally the Jats were treated as people of a lower order, economically they were considered as the labouring class dependent on the money-lenders. Once freed from the money-lending exploiters–Ch. Chhotu Ram's gift–the Jats had become increasingly assertive, especially politically.

Later, with the Govt. of India's emphasis on the modernization of agriculture in the post-Independence era, the Jat and other farming communities had become increasingly prosperous, at least those with large land-holdings. So much so, that gradually, especially after their conversion to Arya Samaj, they had come to acquire a sense, not only of equality with the upper castes, but also of superiority over them, since the Brahmans and Banyas were in the minority in the villages, and were mostly without lands – no Baniya and not many Brahmans owned lands. All these factors combined to make the Jats more and more assertive, giving them the kind of feeling the Jat-Sikhs entertained in Punjab–that the state belonged to them, and it was for them to rule.

Now, since that feeling had been hurt, the Jats in November 1966 were smarting like the wounded lion waiting to pounce back at the enemy. The opportunity soon came; the election to the State Assembly in 1967 was announced within weeks of the formation of the first Government of Haryana headed by Pandit Bhagwat Dayal Sharma. The Jats tried to secure a majority of seats by defeating the non-Jat candidates in the constituencies of their dominance, voting for the non-Congress Jat candidates. In caste arithmatic, the Jats secured the numerical majority, for, even within the Congress, they were the single-caste majority. But their aspirations to capture power were once again thwarted by the Congress High Command when Pandit Bhagwat Dayal Sharma was again made the Chief Minister of the state. This, they felt, was too much. And the revolt came within months of the formation of the new Government of Haryana; the Jats combined with the land-owning legislators of the other castes–Ahirs, Gujars, Rors, etc., and brought down Pandit Bhagwat Dayal Sharma's government.

When it came to deciding the question of leadership, the Jats among the rebel legislators, though numerically more than the rebels from any other caste, were not able to agree on any name. The Jats are traditionally known for their aversion to accepting any other from the community as their superior, each considering himself better than the other. Besides, none among them in that year was exceptionally rich to establish his superiority. As a result, Rao Birender Singh of Rewari, the grand son of Rao Tula Ram, having royal credentials and being monetarily superior to any other contender, succeeded in securing the Chief Ministership of Haryana.

A Jat leader, Ch. Shri Chand, a nephew of Ch. Chhotu Ram, was made the Speaker. To appease the other stalwarts – Ch. Hardwari Lal, Ch. Partap Singh Daulta, Ch. Khurshid Ahmed, etc. – the Rao had to include in his Cabinet a large number of legislators. In fact, almost every member of the rebellious flock got either a ministerial berth or an equivalent cosy position. This was the largest Cabinet the state of Haryana has ever had since its inception

And yet, the government of Rao Birender Singh could not complete one year; it fell within months. History provides ample evidence to the pattern that the rebels or conspirators of different hues remain together only so long as their aim of killing or deposing the common enemy is not achieved; the moment their aim is achieved, they start falling apart. Those who killed Julius Caesar did not stick together for long. Nor did even Antony and Octavius, who had defeated the killers of Caesar.

It may not be wrong to say that men fall for power just as quickly as they do for women, and no man tolerates a rival for a woman or a crown. History keeps repeating itself. But when was that ever a lesson to the power-hungry individuals? They have been rising and falling as inevitably as the sun, and they will go on rising and falling in future in the same way. For " 'Tis in ourselves that we are thus or thus", as says Iago, the villain, in Shakespeare's *Othello* (Harrison, 1067).

The rise and fall of the non-Congress government in Haryana was not an isolated phenomenon. In 1967, several states of the Indian Union, including Punjab, Uttar Pradesh, Bihar, and West Bengal, saw the phenomenon of rebellion within the Congress Party, with the splinter group combining with the opposition parties to form a non-Congress government. These governments came to be called *Samyukt Vidhayak Dal* Governments. The elements in the combination being heterogeneous, no one expected them to remain together for long, except, of course, in the case of West Bengal where the elements were not so heterogeneous, all being followers of the Marxist ideology.

In fact, the case of West Bengal is unique in that while all other non-Congress governments formed in 1967 fell within months, the Communist Government in West Bengal has remained in place for these forty years (except for the interruption in 1972 when the election was rigged by the Congress Government at the Centre, installing an unpopular government headed by Shri Siddharth Shankar Ray, who was also instrumental in the imposition of Emergency in the entire country in 1975, the consequences of which are too well-known to be repeated here.

Without expressing belief in the superstition, we cannot ignore the fact that the odd number of seven in every decade has been lucky for the non-Congress combinations in the States as well as at the Centre. We know how most States of the Indian Union were again blessed with the non-Congress governments in the year 1977. It was for the first time after Independence that the Central Government at Delhi was formed by the non-Congress combination called the Janata Party. In the next decade also, history repeated itself in 1987, with the non-Congress parties capturing power in several states including Haryana, followed by the non-Congress Government at the Centre in 1989 headed by Shri V.P. Singh. The odd number seven caused the First War of Independence in 1857 and brought freedom to India in 1947.

But both in 1977 and 1987, just as in 1967, the non-congress government did not last the full term of five years. Except for West Bengal, all other states saw their earlier histories repeated, making way for the Congress governments in 1991 both at the Centre as well as in Haryana. In the next decade of the 1990's, the change came about in Haryana as well as at the Centre one year earlier, in 1996, rather than 1997, because of the early election in 1991. Otherwise, the lucky number of seven, lucky for the non-Congress parties, would have continued to favour them. It did favour them again in 1996, bringing back the non-Congress governments at the Centre as well as in Haryana and Punjab.

To get back to Haryana, the elections were held again in 1968, within a year of the election of 1967. Since the non-Congress combination could not remain in place for long, people again opted for the single-party government of the Congress. Wiser from the fall of the Bhagwat Dayal Sharma government, the Congress Party decided to have its Chief Minister from the majority caste of the Jats. The Party did not want to continue with the experiment that had failed twice– the experiment of having a Chief Minister from a caste other than the one in the majority. Theoretically, majoritarianism may not be desirable in a democracy, but practically, there has been no alternative to this successful practice.

This political philosophy of handing over power to the majority community the Congress Party had already experimented with in Punjab. We know how the governments of the non-Sikh Chief Ministers, Shri Bhim Sen Sachar, Dr. Gopi Chand Bhargav, and Comrade Ram Kishan, had met with the same fate as that of Pandit Bhagwat Dayal Sharma's Government. Similarly, Haryana was given a government headed by a Jat Chief-Minister, Jats being, like the Sikhs in Punjab, more politically motivated and more power-oriented than any other caste or community, besides their being a majority caste.

The question of choosing a leader is, however, always handled tactfully in the Congress Party. One of the tried tricks of the Congress Party is that of never announcing the leader before or during the election; rather, it creates an illusion of there being a strong possibility for every contender, thereby capturing the vote-banks of more than one major caste or community in the state. In the Haryana Assembly election of 1968, Sh. Hemvati Nandan Bahuguna, being the General Secretary incharge of Haryana affairs, was assigned the delicate job of keeping all contenders in the greenfield, cleverly devising a formula for the elimination of the non-Jat heavy weight, Pandit Bhagwat Dayal Sharma.

Sh. Bahuguna's shrewdness, an asset for the Congress Party, proved a liability for himself, for it was this very shrewdness which was perceived as a threat by the High Command – an euphism in the Congress Party's idiom for the Party President – leading to his ouster from the party he had served so long. The ouster came, of course, a long time after the Haryana election of 1968. After his exit from the Congress during the Emergency in mid 1970's, Shri Bahuguna joined the Lok Dal headed by Ch. Charan Singh, becoming the party's Vice President.

During the years of this writer's membership of the Haryana Assembly (1982-87), Sh. Bahuguna was still in the Lok

Dal as Ch. Charan Singh's deputy. Once while talking about the election of 1968, he told this writer how he had successfully kept Pandit Bhagwat Dayal Sharma away from the seat of power. Using the political skill he had acquired over the long years of experience as an important functionary in the Congress Party's organisation, Sh. Bahuguna succeeded in convincing Pandit Bhagwat Dayal Sharma that the latter should not contest the Assembly election because as the tallest leader of the Congress Party's Haryana unit he would be required to canvass in all the constituencies of the state.

Flattery being the weakness of men in power, or of even those out of power, Pandit Ji soon fell for the vainglory of the mirror image. He must have imagined himself moving across the length and breadth of the state, drawing crowds in every corner, carrying his message home to stamp it on the ballet paper, to regain the crown earlier usurped by the rowdy rebels. Sh. Bahuguna's bait worked, keeping the Pandit–a Haryanvi, after all–out of the contest for the leadership of the legislative party as well.

Disenchanted as the people of Haryana were with the non-Congress parties, and united as the Congress remained, despite the strong antipathy between Pandit Bhagwat Dayal Sharma and the Jat leaders, as also between the castes the two factions represented, the Congress Party won the election with a comfortable majority. Here was once again a testing time for the man assigned the job to install a Jat Chief Minister. Sh. Bahuguna then conjured up another trick. He came to the state party legislators with a directive from the High Command that the leader of the legislative party was to be elected from among the elected representatives of the people.

Pandit Bhagwat Dayal Sharma felt cheated by the High Command's directive, but he did not have enough support to stage a coup. Also, he was offered another illusion, that being taller than others in the Congress Party's Haryana unit, he now belonged to the nation and, therefore, would be accommodated at the Centre to help guide the destiny of the developing nation. Illusions work wonders in politics, perhaps anywhere. This one certainly did. The Pandit cooperated with his senior in seeking a suitable alternative to his leadership

The next trial for the High Command's mediator, Sh. Bahuguna, was to select a suitable state lieutenant for the Central Authority. Since the question of the caste royal had already been decided, the only point to be pondered was who among the Jats would foot the bill. Considering the seniority, the loyalty, and the honesty of Ch. Ranbir Singh Hooda, Shri H.N. Bahuguna considered him most suitable to head the Congress government in Haryana. But there was in store for Shri Bahuguna the surprise of surprises: Ch. Ranbir Singh excused himself saying that he was not cut out for the tricky task of managing the unmanageable, the foxy flock of Haryana legislators. There may not be another example of such a politician as Ch. Ranbir Singh who spurned the grand offer with such simplicity.

Ch. Ranbir Singh was rightly wary of his elected fellows, for he had watched the drama during the murky year of 1967, when legislators changed sides by the day, even by the hour - one M.L.A. changed the party lebel three times in a day - earning the dubious distinction of "Aya Ram, Gaya Ram" – that is how the then Governor of the new state of Haryana, Sh. B.N. Chakravarti, had described the lot of Haryana legislators in his report to the President of India. It was on the basis of this Report that the Haryana Assembly was dissolved in 1967. Being a gentle and quiet sort, Ch. Ranbir Singh did not want to get into a game he had never played. His politics had been clean, and he did not want to take the risk of soiling it.

Since in the choice of the leader of the legislative party at the time Pandit Bhagwat Dayal Sharma was also to consent, the man who thought he had been deprived of his due, as also Shri Gulzari Lal Nanda, the senior most leader from Haryana at the Centre, besides being a leader of the Punjabi community in the new state–a community more modern at the time in more ways than the native communities of Haryana – Ch. Bansi Lal emerged as a dark horse, considered by the two leaders Sh. Bahuguna consulted as the "most humble" of the lot, having not much following among the MLA's or the people. From his appearance, he looked more of a Bania than a Jat. It is another matter though that the "most humble" Jat, the dark horse, turned out soon to be the toughest customer the duo of Pandit Bhagwat Dayal Sharma and Sh. Gulzari Lal Nanda could have expected. They discovered to their utter dismay that the dark horse they had chosen was a dangerous one.

The case of Ch. Bansi Lal proved the remark Dr Sarup Singh once made about a Professor at Kurukshetra, considered very meek and humble. Dr Singh's comment was, "you give him the power of headship of the department and see how he would bloom into a tyrant overnight." Being a close friend of Ch. Bansi Lal, Dr. Sarup Singh would not have directly said the same thing about the former that he had said about the Professor. Decidedly, Shri Bahuguna was not a successful reader of the Jats, nor a successful dealer in this difficult species.

So, the man picked up by Sh. Bahuguna and approved by Sh. Gulzari Lal Nanda and Pandit Bhagwat Dayal Sharma, finally getting the High Command's nod, was Ch. Bansi Lal. Although not one of the key players in Haryana politics at the time, Ch. Bansi Lal was not quite new to the state politics. Before he became the Chief Minister, he had been elected to the state Assembly in 1967 and 1968, and had been a member of the Rajya Sabha from 1962 to 1967.

During this short period in politics, Ch. Bansi Lal had developed political contacts with certain important people in the Congress Party, including Sh. Uma Shankar Dixit of U.P. and Sh. Gulzari Lal Nanda and Pandit Bhagwat Dayal Sharma. These contacts helped him to become the Chief Minister of Haryana. The present Chief Minister of Delhi, Smt. Shiela Dixit, incidentally, is the daughter-in-law of Sh. Uma Shankar Dixit, a close confidant of Smt. Indira Gandhi in the 1960s and 1970s.

Ch. Bansi Lal's affiliation with Pandit Bhagwat Dayal Sharma was so well known that when the Jats were plotting to topple Pandit Bhagwat Dayal Sharma's government soon after its formation in 1967, he was a suspect in the eyes of the plotters who thought that he might not vote with them to bring down the government of the day. In order not to take any risk in this case, they decided that Ch. Bansi Lal should be prevented from reaching the state Assembly on the fateful day.

The man who took the responsibility of preventing Ch. Bansi Lal from reaching the state Assembly that day was Ch. Dharam Pal Singh Rathee, the Chief Conservator of Forests at the time, a member of the Jat Biradi at Chandigarh. As he once told the author, what he did was that he invited Ch. Bansi Lal to his place on some pretext, and when the guest went to use the toilet, the host bolted the toilet door from outside, letting him out only after the plotters had succeeded in voting out the government led by Pandit Bhagwat Dayal Sharma. No wonder when Ch. Bansi Lal took over the reins of power in 1968, the first thing he did was to suspend this officer, and finally to see him out of the government service. The man is still alive and runs a school at Manali.

4

Ch. Bansi Lal's Long Innings 1968-1977

Once out of the stable, the dark horse soon turned a stallion. Ch. Bansi Lal emerged as a strong-willed man, ready to go ruthless to achieve his targets. He went about the job of developing the infrastructure of roads, electricity, industry, schools, etc., connecting every village to state and national highways, lighting every home in every hutment, creating industrial complexes in different parts of the state, especially in the towns surrounding the national capital, creating tourist centers in every district, especially on the routes leading to Agra, Jaipur, Shimla, and Kashmir, putting up schools every seven kilometers or so.

This dynamism that Ch. Bansi Lal displayed, showing results sooner than anyone expected, gave him confidence and created for him a secure place in Haryana politics, so secure that he now started shedding the political load from his shoulders, cutting to size those considered his mentors, including

Sh. Gulzari Lal Nanda, Pandit Bhagwat Dayal Sharma, and Ch. Devi Lal.Wordsworth's utterance, 'The Child is the father of the Man', seems to have as much relevance in politics as it has in nature.

The case of Ch. Devi Lal is interesting. Showing his indebtedness to the senior politician, Ch. Bansi Lal, in his early days as Chief Minister, made Ch. Devi Lal Chairman of the Haryana State Khadi Board. Once while the two were traveling from Chandigarh to Delhi, Ch. Devi Lal tried to impose some suggestion of his on the new Chief Minister who temperamentally had a strong aversion to any imposition, even of a suggestion. When Ch. Devi Lal kept insisting that the Chief Minister must take his advice, Ch. Bansi Lal, in his inimitable style, asked the driver to stop and showed his senior the door, dropping him on the road-side.

As things go in Haryana, the incident soon became a street talk, finally settling in the folk memory as a legend about the strong man of Haryana, Ch. Bansi Lal. A man gifted with the ability to play, if expedient, the role of a court jester, Ch. Sultan Singh, who at that time was the President of Haryana Pradesh Congress Committee, made a convenient use of the incident to humour the master by tickling his vanity. This second incident is all the more interesting.

Once while Ch. Sultan Singh was traveling with the Chief Minister from Chandigarh to Delhi by road, the latter asked him for his opinion on something. In his jester's role, Ch. Sultan Singh said that he would offer his opinion when the car got close to a shady tree. When the Chief Minister asked, how is a tree important in the expression of an opinion, Ch. Sultan Singh's reply was that in case he was dropped on the roadside, he could at least escape the scorching sun by resorting to the shelter of the tree. The joke had its desired effect. The vanity of Ch. Bansi Lal was tickled and he felt immensely satisfied with the company of his entertainer. In fact, it was precisely for this very purpose that Ch. Bansi Lal would generally desire the company of Ch. Sultan Singh on his frequent journeys by road from Chandigarh to Delhi. It made his journeys entertaining, free from stress and boredom.

Once secure in his seat of power, and gradually grown into an intolerant administrator, Ch. Bansi Lal not only parted company with his mentors and well-wishers like Shri Gulzari Lal Nanda, Pandit Bhagwat Dayal Sharma, and Ch. Devi Lal, he started ridiculing them in public speeches. This writer remembers one of his uncharitable remarks about Sh. Gulzari Lal Nanda, regarding his statue at Kurukshetra. Since Sh. Nanda was the one who took up the cause of Kurukshetra's development, especially the historical places connected with the battle of the *Mahabharta* and the gospel of the *Bhagvad Gita*, his admirers had insisted on installing his statue at the Holy Tanks. Ch. Bansi Lal's comment, often quoted those days, was that Sh. Nanda was as good as dead – the reason why his statue was installed while he was still living. Years later, however, Ch. Bansi Lal, in his last stint as Chief Minister (1996-1999), sanctioned a memorial structure for the same leader.

To Pandit Bhagwat Dayal Sharma, too, Ch. Bansi Lal, those days, seldom made a reference without an ironic sting in it. One of his remarks often quoted was that rather than meddle in politics of the state where there was hardly any place left for him,Pandit Bhagwat Dayal Sharma had better turn a "pujari" whereby he could at least make some earning. Not only that, Ch. Bansi Lal sidelined his friends and mentors not subservient in their dealings with him; he went all out to see them either ousted from the Congress Party, or made them redundant in the organization. In the Indian tradition of showing reverence for the dead, Ch. Bansi Lal's attitude to Pandit Bhagwat Dayal Sharma changed after the latter's death.

We know how Ch. Devi Lal as well as Pandit Bhagwat Dayal Sharma, realizing that there was no scope for them for an effective political life in the Congress, had to join the opposition ranks in the 1970's. Sh. Gulzari Lal Nanda, being too strongly committed to the Congress Party, was not the one who would seek an alternate political outfit. Besides, he was in national politics, never a player at the lower level of the state. So he stayed on with his mother–like Congress Party, but remained a persona–non-grata in Haryana during the regime of Ch. Bansi Lal. The one-time disciple had grown into an intolerant ruler.

While Ch. Bansi Lal's treatment of his mentors and friends may be considered shrewd in politics, it was not appreciated by the non-political common people who took it as something unethical. As for Ch. Bansi Lal, the increasing sense of security and confidence made him not only arrogant but also autocratic. As the years piled up of his Chief Ministership, he grew like a Colossus, thinking others would "walk under his huge legs and peep about." Ch. Bansi Lal proved, yet another time, like all men risen to power do, the sagacity of Shakespeare's observation in *Julius Caesar*:

> That lowliness is young ambition's ladder,
> Whereto the climber upward turns his face.
> But when he once attains the upmost round,
> He then unto the ladder turns his back,
> Looks in the clouds, scorning the base degrees
> By which he did ascend. So Caesar may. (Harrison, 822)

Yes, the Haryana's Caesar did just the same. He kicked the ladder – his benefactors – by which he had climbed to the top. However, with all his faults of pride and arrogance, Ch. Bansi Lal did show concrete results in making Haryana a modern state, bringing it at a par with the once big brother Punjab. But as the saying goes, nothing comes without a cost: Development came at the cost of Democracy.

For Ch. Bansi Lal's achievements in the state's economic growth, the price was paid by the institution of democracy which was reduced to a mere form, with levers of power controlled individually by the strong man. All strong men, averse to democracy and its institutions, always rely upon efficient instruments. Ch. Bansi Lal, too, had a team of officers headed by Sh. S.K. Mishra, a son-in-law of Sh. Uma Shankar Dixit, a senior Congress leader close to Smt. Indira Gandhi. The C.M's Chief aid was assisted by Sh. R.P. Mehtani. Bureaucracy, we know, blooms to its full in the reign of autoicracy.

The autocratic style of functioning of Ch. Bansi Lal, combined with the imperial aura of his bureaucratic brigade, alienated him from the masses. Boards and Corporations, Panchayats and Municipalities, even Ministeries of the Govt., came to be managed by figureheads, having no identity of their own with the real power wielded by the top brass. This model of managing the state as a personal fiefdom was not quite new in Haryana. Actually, it was created by Sardar Partap Singh Kairon in the undivided Punjab, who became an example of a strong and successful Chief Minister for the successive incumbents to the seat of power both in Punjab and Haryana. One thing of course must be conceded: Caesar or Coriolanus , Kairon or Bansi Lal, such persons do have some mark of superiority which places them above the rest.

In his first term (1968-72) as Chief Minister, however, Ch. Bansi Lal's sons and daughters were not yet ready to share the task of governance. He functioned through his coterie of a handful of bureaucratic aids – they enjoyed a status similar to that of his own near and dear ones. It was only in his second term (1972-75) that his younger son, Ch. Surinder Singh, had emerged as a proactive younger partner in the business of governance, reducing the administration to an organization of his own. A little later, his middle daughter, Mrs. Saroj Siwach, had joined them to share part of the burden of running the government of the small state.

Ch. Bansi Lal may have been the first to copy Sardar Partap Singh Kairon as a political model: later the model as such became the order of the day in both the states, with all those who came to rise to that position, unofficially allowing their kith and kin to confiscate the powers of their own Cabinet colleagues. Today, the model has become a practice in all states of the Indian Union, with hardly a leader not grooming his son or daughter to function as his heir-apparent in managing the party politics as well as the government administration. Some parties, such as the CPM and CPI, do, of course, remain an exception to the rule; their Chief Ministers have to work in a system.

Returning to Ch. Bansi Lal, though he was picked up as Chief Minister for his caste credentials as a Jat, he turned to the non-Jat legislators, officers, and others for mobilizing support in the Assembly, as well as the administration. Perhaps, he had to do it because he saw in the Jat leaders a threat to his top position. Also, perhaps he had to establish his secular credentials in the Congress Party, which would lose its votebank if tainted with casteism. Further, perhaps he was not a casteist in the mould of the Zamidar League, and had a secular thinking of his own. Even while the last reason is granted, the pressures of the Congress culture and its caste composition, combined with the threat of the ambitious Jat leaders, could not be ignored as Ch. Bansi Lal's compulsions for wooing the non-Jats. Of course, the smaller fries among the Jats stuck to him, just as this stuff would stick to anyone in the seat of power. No wonder he used to call Ch. Devi Lal's followers as *Lath Dal* – that pleased the non-Jats immensely.

This maiden term of Ch. Bansi Lal as Chief Minister earned him the title of the ardent doer, the inflexible administrator, and the maker of modern Haryana, changing the state from a backward region into a developed state, with water and electricity, roads and transport, schools and colleges, hospitals and health - centers, tourist hubs and rest - houses, planned townships and paved villages. His maiden term was, however, cut short when Smt. Indira Gandhi declared election for Parliament in early 1972, with Haryana finding it expedient to have its election held simultaneously with that of the Parliament. Otherwise, the election to the Haryana state Assembly was due in 1973.

Riding the wave of victory over Pakistan in the war that began in the closing weeks of 1971, in which about one hundred thousand army-men of Pakistan surrendered after losing the entire territory of East Pakistan, Smt. Indira Gandhi knew she would sweep the elections if held soon after the war. Ch. Bansi Lal was quick to take a decision to the same effect, although the election to the State Assembly was due in 1973. Sudden situations and silky slogans have always done wonders in the strange game of politics.

Thus, the politics of Haryana during this short span of four years (1968-72) had a sort of 'Indian Summer', to use an

American expression, when the old antagonism between the Jats and the Brahmans and the Baniyas, the newfound cultural disaffection between the natives and the Punjabis, and the business rivalry between the native merchant-class and the new Punjabi entrepreneurs, went dormant. Except for the minority voice of the Jan Sangh and the mild voice of Ch. Charan Singh's BLD, there was no opposition party with a significant presence in the state. In such a political scenario, it was but appropriate that a person like Ch. Bansi Lal should emerge as the central figure in the state, with no strong liking or disliking for any caste or class, except for individuals not amenable to his domineering personality. It was perhaps the people's and perhaps the political parties, enthusiasm for the new state of their own which negated many a negative drive which normnally activate politics and politicians.

Not that Ch. Bansi Lal faced no challenge in the state. There were some persons made of stubborn stuff who would hate to bend, but they were not in a position to pose any serious threat to his seat of power in the party to which he belonged and the govt. he headed. A few instances about the man's tough methods need to be mentioned here to reveal the nature of his administration. For the 'Indian summer' may have prevailed on the social level in general, but politically speaking, it was only an appearance, not a reality.

To mention a stray scene, once while Ch. Bansi Lal, the Chief Minister of the state, was speaking at a public function in Thaneswar, a young man stood up to say something, but before he could utter his message, whatever that was, half a dozen police constables assaulted him with batons and dragged him away to the police station. What they must have done to him there one can only guess to one's horror. It was this kind of tough message that Ch. Bansi Lal wanted sent to those not prepared to accept his dictatorial style. And he did succeed in sending that message with such treatment as mentioned above to whoever raised his head before him, or even behind him. Some may have admired him, but most feared him for his tough style of functioning.

Another time, in Ch. Bansi Lal's later phase as the Chief Minister of Haryana, a blind old man, Ch. Dharam Singh Rathee, once a member of the Haryana Assembly, spoke at a public function against the atrocities being committed by the local agents of the authority, and in particular against the local Superintendent of Police. In his worked-up mood, the blind old man committed the indiscretion of making unbecoming comments on the private life of the SP's wife. How the SP responded to those comments is a nerve-shaking narrative. It must go on record in the transcript of this narrative.

The local despot called the S.P. got the blind old man arrested, his body thrashed with batons, stripped naked, his face blackened; in his natural attire with unnatural face, the man was paraded through the crowded streets of the small town. It was an appalling instance of human apathy that the thousands who saw the spectacle remained cool and quiet, showing no sign of outrage, expressing no opinion in public or press. We heard of it all the next day. An equally wonderful truth about the human race is that there always come up some individuals who stand above the rest and stir the conscience of the teeming millions.

Here, in this particular situation, the man above the rest was Ch. Devi Lal, who, although belonging to a far-off place in the present district of Sirsa, came all the way to arouse the humanity of the local population. Being a political leader of long standing, though never the Chief Minister of the state, his name was familiar to all those given to reading or hearing news through the media. The intensity of terror was so deep in the small town of Thanesar that no one would even rent Ch. Devi Lal the loud-speaker for publicity to the effect that he was organizing a protest meeting the next day against the local authorities for the inhuman treatment meted out to the blind old man.

But brave as Ch. Devi Lal was, undaunted by any authority, he got hold of an empty can and a small wooden stick and went through the town streets announcing his plan for a protest meeting. It inspired a good number of people who joined his protest rally the next day, exposing the wrong doings of the administration, local as well as national, ending the rally with a march through the main bazar of the town. The event may not have raised a storm, but it did stir the conscience of many a middling man.

With this scenario of long silence in the state, the Congress Party had rightly left to the custody of Ch. Bansi Lal the affairs of the party as well as the state. Of course, formally or nominally, there was Ch. Sultan Singh as President of the State Congress Committee, but he was the most convenient party-head any Chief Minister would wish to have. With no following among the masses, neither heading any group in the party, nor having any aristocratic or feudal background, he was utterly dependent on the Chief Minister for his bread and butter as well as for retaining his appointment.

With not much lands in his possession, nor any education to recommend himself, Ch. Sultan Singh had started as a *sewak* of Ch. Ranbir Singh, who himself held high positions in the state or at the Center, such as a Cabinet Minister in the state Govt. or a Member of Parliament in Delhi. Artful as Ch. Sultan Singh is in many ways, he gradually became those days an almost a member of Ch. Ranbir Singh's family, so much so that the two came to constitute in the public mind a sort of duo. Given to serving the powers that be, however, Ch. Sultan Singh parted company with his benefactor and chose to serve whoever succeeded in occupying the seat of power, so much so that when Ch. Om Parkash Chautala assumed power in 1999, the serving gentleman said goodbye to the Congress Party for greener pastures of the new government.

Politics is a strange game, indeed. When you are a winner, it makes you vain. When you are a loser, you seek desperate means to retrieve your lost territory. In either case, your tendency is to be less than fair to others. In victory, you treat others as pigmies, much smaller than your own size. In defeat, you take to foxy ways to rout your rivals by deceit. Very few take the straight path to mix with the masses for gaining political power. Even noble persons turn proud and partial. Those not so noble turn outright despots and unjust. That is when you are in power; when out of power, you pretend humility, showing spurious meekness.

Ch. Bansi Lal, once seeming meek and humble, had amply proved, soon after his ascendence to power, that he was a hard nut to crack. The seat of power to such a person is more precious than any pearl, dearer than any darling. Ch. Bansi Lal loved KURSI (Chair) no less. He was fond of openly pronouncing that he hailed from a region (*Bagar*) where people once on the camel back would not come down, however unfriendly the animal might turn; they would retain their hold on the animal even hanging by its tail. As for the KURSI, the seat of power, he would say, there was no question of quitting, leaving it for someone else, come what may. In other words, no holds bar in the business of retaining power.

Ch. Bansi Lal's remark may sound crude, but it is pregnant with deep truth about the constitution of those committed to power politics, not to social ideals, leave aside the moral or the ethical goals. A supreme illustration of the remark was soon to follow. In her election from Rai Braley in 1972, one of Smt. Indira Gandhi's rivals was Shri Raj Narain, a socialist, an ardent follower of his mentor, Sh. Ram Manohar Lohia, a founding father of the Socialist Party. Shri Raj Narain was as theatrical in his public postures as was his master. Having lost the election to Parliament, Sh. Raj Narain had filed an election petition in the Allahabad High Court of U.P. The case went on for quite a while, as usual. The technical ground was that Shri Yashpal Kapoor, a government officer, had been spotted arranging a *shamiana* for an election meeting of Smt. Indira Gandhi. Seemingly a frivolous charge, it was enough in the language of law to unseat even the mightiest of the mighty politicians. And so it did. In 1974, the election of Smt. Indira Gandhi to Parliament was declared void.

Although a small state, hardly known for producing national leaders in any field, Haryana has not remained behind in producing some very fine human beings who followed the dictates of their conscience and remained above board despite their long span of forty or fifty years in politics. The generation that took part in the freedom struggle had a galaxy of such local leaders, including Bhagat Phool Singh, Ch. Ranbir Singh Hooda, Pandit Sri Ram Sharma, Professor Sher Singh, Ch. Devi Lal, to name only a few of that generation. They, too, were in politics alongside those that earned the state the dubious title of Aya Ram, Gaya Ram.

Professor Sher Singh, a member at the time in the Union Cabinet, was among the first who strongly resented Mrs. Indira Gandhi's not following the moral convention of resigning after losing her seat in the Parliament. Others who shared his anguish included Shri Chander Sekhar, Shri Krishan Kant, Shri Mohan Dharia, and Shri Ram Dhan. A meeting was held at Prof. Sher Singh's official residence on Motilal Nehru Marg which was attended by forty three M.P.'s. One of these forty three resenting members, Shri Prakash Vir Shastri, is said to have played the black sheep; he informed Mrs. Gandhi about the decision the M.P.'s had taken at the meeting – they had decided to ask her to step down, failing which the group would take an appropriate step, but at no cost would they make any compromise on the issue of her resignation from the post of Prime Ministership (Singh, 123-126).

Known for her decisiveness, Smt. Indira Gandhi quickly declared Internal Emergency, putting behind bars, first of all, the 8 of those 43 M.P.'s who had met at Professor Sher Singh's residence, the other thirty five having chosen the wiser course of seeking peace with Smt. Gandhi by expressing their loyalty to her. Thousands of other leaders and activists of different parties were arrested and sent to jails during the Emergency. Those arrested in Haryana included, besides Prof. Sher Singh, several political leaders, such as Ch. Devi Lal (BLD), Dr Mangal Sein (Jan sangh), Shri. Raghubir Singh Hooda (CPM), Shri Mani Ram Bagri (Socialist), Sant Hardwari Lal, Balwant Rai Tayal (Congress O), Babu Mool Chand Jain. The full list need not be mentioned here.

Even student leaders were not spared during the Emergency: Shri Prithvi Singh, Sh. Inderjit, Sh. Balbir Singh Dahiya, Sh. Sradhanand Solanki, Shri Devinder Sharma, Shri Roshan Lal Arya were among the more prominent ones who were put behind bars. Even the Arya Smaj leaders like Swami Agnivesh, Swami Indervesh, Swami Shaktivesh had to share the same fate. Leaders of the Haryana School Teachers Union, including Shri Sohan Lal, Shri Shanti Rathee, Shri Ran Singh Maan, Master Bhale Ram, etc., were also sent to jail. Leaders of the College Teachers' Association were also not spared; Shri Samarjit Singh, Shri Rati Ram, and Shri Teja Singh, along with some more teachers were taken into custody. Then a large number of the RSS cadre, too, were sent to jail, a prominent one among whom was Sh. Shyam Khosla, a regular Staff Correspondent with *The Tribune*.

The style of the state administration in Haryana was despotic and arbitrary, crude and cruel. Ch. Surinder Singh, Ch. Bansi Lal's younger son, got arrested even those who had, as members of an examination flying squad of Kurukshetra University, not allowed students to copy in the examinations. Dr P.C. Jain of the Economics Department and Dr Surinder Chopra of Political Science, both from Kurukshetra University, were among the victims of this category. The atrocities were unlimited and, as it seemed, unending. The Emergency rule permitted all that.

Smt. Indira Gandhi was in no mood to vacate the seat of power. She would rather hang on to it even by the tail, so to say. Not Ch. Bansi Lal and his fellow *Bagris* alone, others in politics would do the same when it came to quitting the cosy seat of power. Rather than accept the court verdict, Smt. Indira Gandhi, on the advice of her coterie, which also included Ch.

Bansi Lal, had preferred the measure of Emergency, overriding the powers of the democratic institutions, placing in prison all leaders of the various political parties, big or small, enjoying local, regional, or national status.

The people of India were taken aback, not knowing for quite a while how to take the unprecedented measure the desperate person(s) in power had resorted to. The common people were not quite used to the new conditions, living as they had been for over a quarter of a century in the environment of a democracy, however feudal in its essential frame. But here was a new reality, mean and monstrous, which could not be wished away. Harsh measures followed to tighten the administrative grip on the people, denying them their democratic rights, not sparing even the fundamental ones. It is hard to forget a statement the Attorney General at the time had officially made in the Apex Court that the police was within its right to shoot anyone it considered undesirable for any reason (without inviting any trial or punishment, intolerable in a civilized state). One could imagine what the country was in for!

Such conditions as the Emergency created were best suited to a man like Ch. Bansi Lal. He could bloom into a harsh ruler permitting his officers to rule ruthlessly and crush the inconvenient. A sort of terror was let loose on whoever spoke to express dissent, indicating disapproval of whatever was happening in the state, even at the local level in a town or district. The local authorities, too, assumed the same hauteur the Central or State authorities had assumed. Instances of the time are innumerable, but some are hard to erase from the memory. To narrate even those few will, however, digress us from our immediate task of mapping the power politics of Haryana.

Between 1972 and 1977, four personalities, though not a serious threat to the dominant position of Ch. Bansi lal, remained in the reckoning for power. Two of these, Professor Sher Singh and Pandit Bhagwat Dayal Sharma, though involved in activities at the national level, remained tall public figures who could not be wished away from the political arena of Haryana. Professor Sher Singh remained a central minister in Smt. Indira Gandhi's Cabinet right from 1967 upto the time of Emergency, when he joined the rebellious band along with Sh. Chander Sekhar, and finally landed in the opposition camp. So did Pandit Bhagwat Dayal Sharma, whom Ch. Bansi Lal was only too happy to see out of the Congress Party. But the proud Chief Minister was unmindful of the ground the two were gaining among the people of Haryana, especially Professor Sher Singh who had shown the courage that had marked his career right from the beginning, to quit his Cabinet berth and join the struggle for restoring Democracy in the country. This was the second time he had sacrificed his position of power; earlier, he had quit the Deputy Chief Minsitership of Punjab when Sardar Partap Singh Kairon was the Chief Minsiter. Not many players of power politics in Haryana can claim such a distinction.

The other two personalities giving uneasy time to Ch. Bansi Lal were Ch. Devi Lal and Ch. Bhajan Lal. While the former, in keeping with his simple and straightforward character, posed a challenge to the all powerful Ch. Bansi Lal from outside, the latter (Ch. Bhajan Lal) emerged, through his subtle and surreptitious ways, as a challenge within the government itself. While between 1968 and 1972, Ch. Bhajan Lal, a first-time legislator, consolidated his position in the power politics, between 1972 and 1977, he had emerged a threat to Ch. Bansi Lal. Even a senior minister, next only to the Chief Minister, Ch. Bhajan

Lal, had to face raids on his business and charges on his person, including that of rape. The assault on the rival only betrayed the magnitude of the threat Ch. Bansi Lal felt from Ch. Bhajan Lal.

While Ch. Devi Lal was put in prison right when the Emergency was declared in 1975 and was kept there for all the nineteen months of the dark period, Ch. Bhajan Lal, pushed to the wall, joined in the last leg of the Emergency period the bandwagon of Babu Jagjivan Ram, a leader of national stature, who, feeling humiliated in the Emergency set-up dominated by a coetrie of upstarts (such as Sh. Siddhartha Shankar Ray and Ch. Bansi Lal) who surrounded Smt. Indira Gandhi, had formed his own political party called the Congress for Democracy.

Still another personality in opposition to Ch. Bansi Lal was Dr. Mangal Sein of the Jan Sangh, whose following was quite substantial in the state of Haryana. A migrant from Pakistan, Dr Sein was a staunch follower of the RSS ideology, and a senior member of the Jan Sangh. Right from the days when Sardar Partap Singh Kairon was the Chief Minister of Punjab in the 1950's, Dr Mangal Sein was an active opponent to the Congress ideology, always fighting for the causes of Hindi and the Hindus. He remained the tallest leader of the migrant Punjabis who settled in Haryana after the Partition of 1947.

When Punjabi was made a compulsory language in the schools in the late 1950's, Dr. Mangal Sein was another leader in the Haryana region, besides Professor Sher Singh, who spearheaded the movement for the protection of the claims of the Hindi language, fiercely resisting the imposition of Punjabi on the Hindi-speaking people. Soon after the Partition of 1947, Punjabi and Hindi had come to be viewed, thanks to the Akalis, as the language respectively of the Sikhs and the Hindus. Since the Akalis were fighting for the creation of Punjabi Suba, as a measure to diffuse the movement, Sardar Partap Singh Kairon had introduced Punjabi as a compulsory language for seeking jobs in the public sector. The measure did not appease the Akalis, but it decidedly antagonized the Hindus.

In fact, it was at this juncture that the duo pleading Haryana's cause – Professor Sher Singh and Ch. Devi Lal – and the Jan Sangh of the Haryana region led by Dr Mangal Sein had come close to each other to form a combined force against the Akali politics and fight for the rights of the Hindus. This combination, after the bifurcation of Punjab into Punjab and Haryana in 1966, consolidated between 1972 and 1977 into an anti-Congress front, mainly spearheaded by Ch. Devi Lal and Dr Mangal Sein. Professor Sher Singh continued to be considered, even in the Janata outfit, a leader of the Congress faction headed by Shri Morarji Desai. Hence he was not considered a part of the anti-Congress force in Haryana's Power politics.

Gradually, Dr Mangal Sein emerged as an undisputed leader of the Punjabi-speaking Hindus in Haryana as well as of the state's Jan Sangh unit. Dr Sein was one of the leading personalities of Haryana arrested when the Emergency was declared. Being an articulate orator, he could always arouse people's passions for matters related to religion and community – a gift not possessed at the time by any of the local Haryana leaders, including Ch. Devi lal, and Professor Sher Singh. Ch. Bansi Lal was never known for such acquisitions. Only Ch. Om PArkash Chautala showed that talent when he came into prominence in the 1990's among the living contenders for power in the state. Sh. Chautala remains the most effective orator among the leading politicians of Haryana even today.

Finding the tiger-ride of the Emergency rather troublesome, as also duped by her own intelligence services, making her believe that if elections were held in the early months of 1977, she was sure to win and form the government again, Smt. Indira Gandhi declared elections to the national Parliament. Since elections were also due for several state Assemblies, simultaneous elections were organized in Haryana as well as certain other states along with the election to Parliament. The various political parties, national as well as regional, decided to merge into one national party, for otherwise, they realized, there was absolutely no scope for any single party, or for even a combination of two or three, to face the might of Smt. Indira Gandhi, especially when she had, as an instrument, the administrative machinery of all the states under her control. But the iron lady of Indian politics had no idea that the silent (or silenced) mass would burst into a volcano of anger and overwhelm the murky machinery which is always quick to change sides for its survival.

In the state of Haryana, the new national political outfit named the Janata Party, which had emerged from the hurriedly cobbled combination of all the national and regional parties of different hues, including the red and the saffron, the green and the blue; the personalities in the forefront included Ch. Devi Lal, Dr Mangal Sein, Professor Sher Singh, Ch. Chand Ram, Pandit Bhagwat Dayal Sharma, and Ch. Bhajan Lal. So, when the election to the state Assembly was declared, it were these leaders who received importance, though, of course, not all in equal measure. Since Haryana was considered a Jat majority state, Ch. Charan Singh, as the new arrangement worked in the Janata Party, called the shots, and the Chaudhary's natural choice for leading the state government was Ch. Devi Lal, others being essentially Congressmen, considered close to Sh. Morarji Bhai Desai, Babu Jagjivan Ram, etc., hence not worthy of the Chaudhary's trust.

What had developed as an underground swell against the repressive regime of the Emergency, suddenly, once the elections were declared, became a whirlwind, a storm that swept the entire northern belt of the country from Kashmir to Calcutta, subsiding only in the South where the measure of the Emergency was perhaps less severe, rather mild, being the farthest pocket from the epicenter of power in Delhi. As we know, fortune smiled broadly on the Janata Party, with the new party making a clean sweep in the North, leaving only one or two seats for the mighty Congress.

In Haryana, only three Assembly seats out of ninety went to the party of the ruthless ruler of the state, Ch. Bansi Lal. Interestingly, all the three went to the young Jat leaders – Ch. Birender Singh (the grandson of Ch. Chhotu Ram) from Uchana, Ch. Samsher Singh Surjewala from Narwana, and Ch. Surinder Singh (son of Ch. Bansi Lal) from Tosham. These survivals were owing to the personal popularity of these upcoming leaders of the dominant caste; their strong hold on their respective electorate was a measure of their individual equation with the people. Ch. Bansi Lal himself lost badly in the parliamentary constituency of Bhiwani. His opponents – Professor Sher Singh and Pandit Bhagwat Dayal Sharma – won with huge margins from the constituencies of Rohtak and Karnal respectively.

The case of Ch. Surinder Singh among the three young Jat leaders is a little intriguing, for he was the most talked-about youth leader of the Congress, along with Sh. Sanjay Gandhi, who had come to symbolize the arbitrary and autocratic style of functioning of the Emergency regime in the state. More than the father, the son had earned a name for the measure of repression let loose on the people of the small state. The potent reason, perhaps, for the surprise win of Ch. Surinder Singh was his partisan treatment given to the people of his own constituency, who received all sorts of favours, while others were not only deprived of their legitimate rights but were discriminated against blatantly and given the stick on the slightest provocation.

Also, while Ch. Bani Lal remained busy with the affairs of the state and the national politics, holding the powerful portfolio of the Defence Minister of India, Ch. Surinder Singh had developed close affinity with the people of Bhiwani, making his home district the sole arena of his service to the people. Besides, he was the defacto Chief Minister of Haryana, Lala Banarsi Dass being only a figure head. The other two young Jat leaders won because they had no hand in whatever had happened during the hard days of the Emergency. Only the duo of Ch. Bani Lal and Ch. Surinder Singh had ruled the state with an iron hand, leaving no role for any other Congressmen, much less for those considered rivals to the father or the son. The Chief Minister at the time, Shri Banarsi Dass Gupta, was a dummy, wholly dominated by Ch. Surinder Singh.

Ch. Devi Lal, after a long struggle of more than half a century in politics, had got in 1977 the well-earned chance of heading the government of Haryana. His long political innings had been full of agitations and revolts, as he seldom chose to settle for a soft life of personal promotion; rather, he had always chosen the difficult path of siding with the subaltern, especially the peasants, raising their demands in and outside the state Assembly, organizing protests, never minding the prison.

Remaining for so long in the politics of opposition to the powers that be, Ch. Devi Lal had hardened his attitude to those who would easily slip or slide into the corridors of power just for a handful of silver or a badge to stick on the shoulder. In a way, Ch. Devi Lal earned the popularity of Ch. Chhotu Ram through a route different from the one his senior had chosen, although their goals remained similar, and so remained similar their stature. So when Ch. Devi Lal was made the Chief Minister of Haryana, he was awarded with something that had been his due for a long time. It was very much a natural choice, given the composition of the mixed breed called the Janata Party in which different groups continued making their respective claims, dividing the dominance of various states among them.

5

Ch. Devi Lal's Populist Regime 1977-1979

When the second non-Congress government was formed in Haryana in 1977, the enthusiasm among the people was as strong as was witnessed after the country's liberation from the British Raj in 1947. Thinking of the significance of the number 7 in India's political history, one realizes how sheer coincidences at times assume the status of destiny. We have before us the crucial historical events of 1947, 1967, 1977, 1987, etc., when poltics in India witnessed major turning points. Going out of themselves, forgetting responsibilities of law and order, the rural folks of Haryana rushed to Chandigarh where the new Govt. was to be sworn in.

The mood of the rural folks from Haryana on the day Ch. Devi Lal was to be sworn in as Chief Minister of the state was what the great comic character in Shakespeare's *Henry IV, Part*

II, describes when his friend Prince Hal is to be coronated as King Henry the Fifth of England. With no means at his command, Falstaff tells his friends to "take any man's horse, the laws of England are at my commandment" (Harrison, 694). so that they can join the ceremony. The enthusiasts from the Haryana villages, the followers of Ch. Devi Lal in particular, were driven by the spirit of Falstaff. They boarded whatever means of transport was at hand, bus or train, truck or tractor, and rushed to Chandigarh.

With crowds descending from all the four sides, Chandigarh soon got submerged into a huge *mela* where all aound one saw only the Haryanvi dresses and heard only the Haryanavi dialects; like a swarm of locusts, the masses descended upon the city, jamming the traffic on the main roads, smashing barricades on their way to the Raj Bhawan, letting loose a sea of turbans and trucks, making the Governor's official residence a Ram Lila *maidan*, where in place of grace and decorum, grossness and defiance ruled.

Ch. Devi Lal was sworn in to head the new government, having in his Cabinet quite a few of those who were not his choice, certainly not his followers, such as Ch. Bhajan Lal, Dr Mangal Sein, Col. Ram Singh, Sh. Balwant Rai Tayal, Smt. Sushma Swaraj, etc. Since the number of Janata Party MLA's was too large to be appeased by their inclusion in the Cabinet, the swearing-in ceremony left disgruntled quite a few. A prominent figure in this lot was Sant Hardwari Lal, who had been a Minister earlier, and was rather proud of his education, considering Ch. Devi Lal and others no match to his merits.

Consequent upon the formation of Ch. Devi Lal's Cabinet, those disgruntled individuals started creating trouble. Sant

Hardwari Lal gave the Chief Minister a hard time. In connivance with his friend, Brigadier Ran Singh, who was the Speaker of the Vidhan Sabha, and Sardar Harcharan Singh Brar, who was the Governor of the state, the Sant (so-called) made embarrassing attacks on the Chief Minister in the House, shaking the latter's confidence. Ch. Devi Lal, then, would be called by the Governor and advised, as planned by Sant Hardwari Lal, to lure the detractor with a plum post so that he could be made to resign his membership of the Assembly. Ch. Udey Singh Dalal, an aspirant to replace Sant Hardwari Lal as member of the Legislative Assembly, also played his part in persuading Ch. Devi Lal to offer Sant Hardwari Lal the Vice-Chancellorship of Maharishi Dayanand University at Rohtak. Finally, the Sant got what he wanted; he became the Vice-chancellor.

Sant Hardwari Lal once gone out of the Assembly, Ch. Devi Lal heaved a sigh of relief. Sant Hardwari Lal had felt had aggrieved and humiliated right from the time he was denied the Janata Party ticket, although he had remained in jail throughout the Emergency period of nineteen months, more ill-treated than any other of his fellow political prisoners. But he won the election from the Badli Assembly constituency of Rohtak district as an independent, defeating Ch. Udey Singh Dalal, the official candidate of the Janata Party.

Denying him an important position in the House was to Sant Hardwari Lal like adding injury to insult. Given his self-pride and volatile temperament, it was but natural that he should quarrel with those in power, bullying them to concede to his demand of accommodation in the world of power and privilege. As an independent member of the Assembly, Sant Hardwari Lal could not be made a member of the Cabinet, there being a large number of the ruling party MLA's. But the Sant could not be content with mere membership of the House. So he manipulated the second best – the Vice–Chancellorship of a university of his choice, that too for an unusual tenure of two statutory terms of three years each.

Simple and straightforward as Ch. Devi Lal was as a person, he had more troubles ahead as the Chief Minister of Haryana. With not much experience of running a government or managing a large crowd of legislators of different hues, he could easily be trapped into making mistakes. Besides, his own followers both in the House as well as in the band of party activists were his worst enemies. This lot was rather unruly, at least quite a few of them. Their unbridled acts of indiscretion alienated Ch. Devi Lal from the bureaucracy in the administration, from his colleagues in the Cabinet, and from the non-Jats among the electorate.

The Janata Party's constituents included the erstwhile Jan Sangh, the Socialists, and the Congress (O). Ill-treated by the Lok Dal rank and file, these fellow constituents started feeling sidelined, even insulted and humiliated. The leaders of the non - Lok Dal Ghataks were treated as aliens by those surrounding the Chief Minister. One incident would do to underline the kind of attitude these tough followers of the rural leader had towards the leaders of their own party–leaders other than those from their own clan.

Once two Ministers of Ch. Devi Lal's Cabinet, Dr Mangal Sein and Smt. Sushma Swaraj, were to halt at the Govt. Rest House at Gohana. This was sometime in 1978 or thereabout, by which time the mistrust between the various factions had acquired some magnitude. These two Ministers, along with certain others in Ch. Devi Lal's Cabinet, had come to be known by then, in the common perception of the Chief Minister's followers, as the dissidents, and were being considered a threat to the supreme position of their leader, Ch. Devi Lal. Shri Blwant Rai Tayal and Ch. Bhajan Lal were among those considered inimical to Ch. Devi Lal.

This lot of Lok Dal (nick named by Ch. Bansi Lal as Lath Dal) knew no means of meeting the challenge of their adversaries except roughing them up. They used the only weapon they knew of at the Gohana Rest House, manhandling Dr Mangal Sein, and not sparing even the female Minister. No self-respecting person could take kindly to such a treatment as was meted out to these two urbanites, not quite familiar with the ways of the followers of their senior Cabinet colleague.

Just within two years of the formation of the Janata Party Govt. of Ch. Devi Lal, the popular support of the legislators had dwindled into a minority of factional followers, with the larger chunk of legislators going about in open defiance or voicing dissent in veiled language. Ch. Bhajan Lal saw an opportunity for a coup. He started mobilizing support from different factions of the ruling party. Three allies were in sight: Pandit Bhagwat Dayal Sharma, the then Governor of Madhya Pradesh; Ch. Chand Ram, a Minister in the central Cabinet of Shri. Morarji Desai; and Dr Mangal Sein, the leader of the Jan Sangh faction in the Janata Party.

Each of these three leaders had a substantial following among the MLA's : Ch. Chand Ram had the largest following of at least fourteen with twelve Scheduled Castes and two Jats – Ch. Mehar Singh Rathee and Smt. Shanti Rathee; Dr Mangal Sein had at least a dozen MLA's with their roots in the RSS; Pandit Bhagwat Dayal Sharma had at least half a dozen of his loyalists. Ch. Bhajan Lal had mustered a following of his own also cutting across the caste boundaries, but mostly the non-Jats. All told, the number rose to forty or so, reducing Ch. Devi Lal's following in the Legislative Party to a clear minority.

Although not an active opponent like Pandit Bhagwat Dayal Sharma, Prof. Sher Singh had also been won over by this combination of various factions. Partly, Ch. Devi Lal's camp was also responsible for this; the band of supporters Ch. Devi Lal had created for himself included rank casteists who had strong distrust of the non-Jat leaders and legislators, especially the Punjabi-speaking people of the state. His followers were by and large the rabid Jats with little sophistication and less sophistry. They were, in short, blunt like bolts.

To a person like Prof. Sher Singh, with his elite education, staunch commitment to the Arya Samaj, and long political life at the Centre, such a following as Ch. Devi Lal had collected for himself could not be acceptable at all; he had nothing to share with this lot. In fact, he, too, had faced rough weather from these followers of the Jat leader whenever he was suspected of supporting (or even having sympathy with) the leader's detractors. Hence, Prof. Sher Singh, too, grouped with the new anti-Devi Lal front of MLA's, MP's, and others.

It was early in 1979, in the last quarter of the second year of Ch. Devi Lal's tenure as Chief Minister, that the drama of *Bharat Darshan* began, which gave to Haryana another first position in the murky politics of India – the earlier first was the practice of *Aaya Ram, Gaya Ram.* Most of the dissident MLA's joined the *Bharat Darshan* tour, sojourning mostly in states where the Jan Sangh faction had its Chief Ministers. Ch. Devi Lal's methods to counter the dissidents' move proved counterproductive. Rather than tempt and woo the distracted lot, his supporters issued threats of not permitting the deserters to enter their constituencies.

Not all went on the *Bharat Darshan*, for the senior leaders of the dissident camp were needed at the headquarters to manage the legalities and political moves for achieving the desired goal of defeating the government of Ch. Devi Lal and replacing it by their own. The rebels on a pleasure-trip or sight-seeing arrived in Chandigarh only on the day of reckoning when the trial of strength was to take place on the floor of the House. They succeeded in achieving what they had planned. The Govt. of Ch. Devi Lal fell when it had just completed two years in office.

As expected, Ch. Bhajan Lal replaced Ch. Devi Lal. Barring the Lok Dal faction, all others joined hands to strengthen the new government. With the support of Pandit Bhagwat Dayal Sharma, Lala Balwant Rai Tayal, Dr Mangal Sein, Ch. Chand Ram, the govt. of Ch. Bhajan Lal was apparently a combination of the non-Jat castes and communities, isolating Ch. Devi Lal as a Jat leader.

The defeated leader gave a call to the people not to welcome the new rulers, encouraging them to use all methods of protest to express their displeasure against the "treacherous" legislators. His appeal incited only his own community, confirming the correctness of the label generally affixed on him, of being a Jat leader. His supporters adopted rough methods, inviting greater displeasure of other castes and communities.

On his part, Ch. Bhajan Lal made frantic attempts to woo the Jat community. Being a first timer as Chief Minister, belonging to a community having insignificant presence in the population of Haryana, the new Chief Minister was not very confident of his position. On the contrary, he had serious apprehensions that without the support of the majority caste of Jats, known for its aggressiveness, it might not be possible for him to run the state administration. He even tried to convince the Jats that he himself was a Jat, for most of those who had converted to the sect of Bishnois were none but Jats themselves.

Despite very hectic efforts, however, Ch. Bhajan Lal could not succeed in winning over the Jats. Rather, the community of Jats turned hostile towards him, taking the toppling of Ch. Devi Lal's government as a community defeat and dishonour. One could often hear people of this community remarking that they had been 'dishonoured' by a Bishnoi, a caste unheard of in Haryana outside the old district of Hisar. To them, it was as deep a shock as a champion wrestler would feel after losing to an upstart or a dark horse hardly known to any lover of the game.

What seemed for a while to have subsided got revived once again, and with a sharper edge: the politics of Jats versus the non-Jats (led by the Brahmans and Buniyas), with its beginnings going back to the time of Ch. Chhotu Ram, got, all of a sudden, revived once again. No wonder Ch. Devi Lal, though an opponent of Ch. Chhotu Ram in his youth, now turned to the revered icon of the community, calling him his mentor, asking the community to revive the same old spirit their leader stood for, and fight against the resurgence of the new combination of the old exploiting communities. In the new polarities of Haryana politics, the Punjabi community of those that came from the East Punjab (now Pakistan) also got grouped with the Brahmans and Baniyas.

Aware of the inadequacy of the single community for winning political power in the state, Ch. Devi Lal raised the slogan of *Kisan* (farmer) unity, making a common cause with the other farming communities of the Ahirs, Rors, Gujars, Sainis, and Rajputs. The move of forming the AJGAR force was also a revival of Ch. Chhotu Ram's politics. To some extent, the Jat leader succeeded in winning large sections of these castes to his side, but the label of his being a Jat leader became unerasable. Despite the call of a grand coalition of the farming communities, however, Ch. Devi Lal's towering figure as a Jat leader did fall short of removing the fear in the non-Jats. Their feeling remained, that once in power, the Jat leader would not give them their due share in the power and privilege the ruling outfit had come to enjoy. The feeling was especially strong among the urban communities and the non-farming castes.

It took many years before Ch. Devi Lal was able to win the complete confidence of the various non-Jat farming communities of Haryana. His move was based on the example Ch. Chhotu Ram and Ch. Charan Singh had set before him–to combine communities having common economic interests. Ch. Chhotu Ram's AJGAR was the tested model. Ch. Devi Lal knew this much of history, and he had learnet the required lesson. As a result, the earlier antagonism of the rural versus the urban, the farmers versus the money-lenders, the natives versus the refugees, got revived. These opposing caste combinations, however, were actually rooted in the clashing class interests determined by the economic structure of the society in the state. Dr. Ram Manohar Lohia's thesis that in India the castes represent classes may have in it a large measure of truth even though it cannot stand the test of a scientific scrutiny.

Once clear in his mind that the Jats would not own him as their own at any cost, Ch. Bhajan Lal, quick as he always is in determining his course of action, started cementing his relations with the non-Jat legislators and communities who were already inclined towards him. The polarization that had started taking shape soon after Ch. Devi Lal took over the reigns of power in 1977 gained consolidation, getting a sharp edge in Haryana politics: the Jats versus the non-Jats, by and large, became the politics of the state, with the two forces, epitomised by their respective leaders, Ch. Devi Lal and Ch. Bhajan Lal, one a simple and solid man of the masses, the other a subtle and sharp man of the moment.

Among other things, Ch. Devi Lal and Ch. Bhajan Lal also came to represent the clash of interests between the farmers and the traders, between the rural masses and the urban elite. These antagonisms are, of course, to be viewed in a general way, on the macro level; for if we go into the minor details of the matter, on the micro level, we shall discover a thousand contradictions in the formulation. But power politics, as we know, is not a subject of details; it is a matter of determining the driving forces that contend to capture the levers of power; it is not a matter of determining which individual, person or community, stood on which side. In fact, more than the factual position, it is the general perception that largely determines the course of power poltics in a society.

Haryana being a small state with the farmers, by and large, owning small land-holdings, and the traders doing small business, with most families, especially in the villages, abjectly waiting for the opportunity to get a govt. job; so much so that the farmers would be ready to sell their lands for securing for their semi-literate or even fully-educated sons such small jobs as that of a constable or a conductor, of a clerk or a cavalryman, even of a peon or a watchman. Quite a few of the rural folk keep running after their local leaders, materially responding to whatever the cogs in the wheel of power demanded.

It is the dire econimic necessity that drives the castes and communities in Haryana to join one or the other camp contending for capturing political power. A popular perception among the people of Haryana has been that while the govt. headed by Ch. Devi Lal would favour the Jats for govt. jobs, the govt. headed by Ch. Bhajan Lal would favour the non-Jats. Among the other benefits that flow from the portals of power, that of joining a govt. job has been the most attractive to the rural folk in Haryana. Such a dependence on the public-sector employmenbt is in much less measure among the urban populace.

Ch. Bhajan Lal, knowing full well what mattered to the people of Haryana, and desperately needing a solid support base in society, tilted the balance towards the non-Jats in doling out jobs to the needy. The privileged ones, the legislators and the likes, would look for more plum positions and profits than securing petty jobs for their supporters. And no one in Haryana knew better than Ch. Bhajan Lal how to go about in the distribution of such favours. So, while he appeased the legislators with fat benefits, he favoured all and sundry in his own constituency. As the popular perception goes, so long as Ch. Bhajan Lal remained the Chief Minister, there was no unemployment in his constituency of Adampur.

These consolidations of castes and communities in deciding the outcome of elections in Haryana led to the creation of what is popularly known as the 'Spoil System', where the elected members to the state Assembly would be amply provided for, strengthening their resources for a permanent position of privilege and influence in the caste-ridden society. This worked very well for Ch. Bhajan Lal, as well as for others who followed in his footsteps, finding no better way for staying in power than adopting the time-tested 'Spoil System.' Gradually, the practice has gained the form of a system which works on certain set principles. The Recruiting Agencies of the state are shaped to serve that system –an example of how Democracy in India has been transformed into a new form of Feudalism.

The said system made the new enterprising Chief Minister quite comfortable. In fact, he soon became popular with certain sections, such as the legislators, the bureaucracy, and all those who hang around in the corridors of power, from the lowest office at the block level to the highest office in the state secretariat; each one of these on the winning side got some gift from the generous head of the new government. It is another matter, though, that when the fortunes of the Chief Minister changed later in 1987, not all of these beneficiaries stayed in his support.

Nothing of this sort is new in the human drama. Both the 'spoil system' as well as the 'system of jilting', in one form or another, have been a part of power politics, whatever be the form of government – Monarchy, Dictatorship, or Democracy. For a time though, so long as the ruler is in place, firmly bottomed in the chair, all goes well. So did it go very well with Ch. Bhajan Lal in the years of his Chiefministership.

But soon came a challenge: the Parliament election of 1980. The combination at the Centre, the combination of several political groups called the Janata Party had crumbled as quickly as the govt. of Ch. Devi Lal. Disparate as it was, highly heterogeneous, it could last only two years, from 1977 to 1979. Ch. Charan Singh, supported by the Socialists, had pulled down in 1979 the Govt. of Shri Morarji Bhai Desai formed in 1977. The party that came in with a bang, went out with a whimper.

The miserably minority Govt. of Ch. Charan Singh survived only a few months with the support of the same Indira Gandhi's Congress Party the Chaudhary and others had humiliated in 1977. Soon the support was withdrawn and the lame-duck Chaudhary's government fell, bringing an early election in 1980. With the return of Smt. Indira Gandhi at the Centre, the non-Congress governments in the states started shaking. But not so the government of Ch. Bhajan Lal. A politician as agile as a gymnast, Ch. Bhajan Lal could weather any storm; he could bend to any form the situation demanded.

In a way, Ch. Bhajan Lal threw a challenge to the old guards in politics, those rooted in the traditional feudal values of personal, or family honour, and of caste or community allegiance. Like the new generation-character named Farfrae in Hardy's *The Mayor of Casterbridge*, Ch. Bhajan Lal could defeat the Henchard-like Ch. Devi Lal on the sheer strength of his being a 'modern' man, and not a traditional man. The old oder changed then giving place to the new. For Ch. Bhajan Lal, political expediency, rather than personal honour, was a more favoured value.

The rise of Ch. Bhajan Lal was a turning point in Haryana's power politics; it marked the end of the Jat dominance. This was no small achievement on the part of Ch. Bhajan Lal. What the non-Jat leaders from Pandit Sri Ram Sharma to Pandit Bhagwat Dayal Sharma could not achieve, despite their long struggle, Ch. Bhajan Lal accomplished in ten years time. This also posed a challenge to the majority community that turned fiercely hostile to him, never relenting in its fury against him. The contest between Ch. Bhajan Lal's foxiness and the Jat fury shaped the power politics of Haryana for over two decades.

6

Ch. Bhajan Lal's Short Maiden Innings 1980-1982

With the change of Governemnt at the Centre, Ch. Bhajan Lal soon changed not only his own stance but also the stance of the entire flock of forty and odd legislators whose following he enjoyed in the State Assembly. The govt. of Ch. Bhajan Lal became overnight a Congress govt. Nothing much seemed to have happened. It was so smooth. Only the change of a word; the word Congress replaced the word Janata.

It is a mark of the remarkable flexibility in our democratic constitution, as well as in our social structure, that there was no stir in any quarter on what had happened. All found it so very normal. Only a few voices in words, or some stray incidents of rural indecencies, and these sounded so odd in the general quiet of our national political life. Not many took note of such little stones thrown into the running stream; the sound of the current of water being so strong that the small noises remained almost unheard.

So Ch. Bhajan Lal's term as Chief Minister remained unshortened, unlike that of his predecessor, Ch. Devi Lal, who in his rurual recalcitrance knew no bending, unable to change with the times. His rival, Ch. Bhajan Lal, proved fitter in the struggle for political survival. *'Gaya Ram, Aya Ram',or 'Aya Ram, Gaya Ram',* though attributed to Haryana, has, in fact, been a normal practice with the bourgeois political parties throughout India. Since the Congress Party was the dominant outfit governing at the Centre as well as in most states of the Union of India, at least until 1977, it continued with the practice of swallowing up the smaller political parties. Right from the time of Pandit Jawahar Lal Nehru, when Ashok Mehta's Socialist Party joined the Congress, this philosophy of growing larger by swallowing the smaller ones had become the main political credo of the ruling party.

Later, the other political parties, like the BJP, whenever and wherever they made it to the seat of power, followed in the footsteps of the Congress. Breaking smaller parties by alluring individuals and groups into the ruling fold has remained a reliable practice with the bourgeois parties in power – at times, even when out of power, they have succeeded in replacing the ruling party through the instrument of alluring. Congress being a small party in U.P and Bihar faces similar situations, with the ruling parties in these states swallowing parts or whole of its legislative unit. The smaller states like Goa witness this farcical drama more often than the larger states like U.P.

Returning to the state of Haryana, realizing once and for all that the dominant community of Jats would not adopt him, Ch. Bhajan Lal went about silently but steadily in consolidating his position among the other castes, especially among the Brahmans and the Punjabis, these two being the major and influential ones in forging a front against the elephantine community of the Jats. Govt. jobs and financial favours, plum positions and discretionary privileges, were distributed to those hailing from these castes, deliberately denying even the due to those belonging to the Jat community that had turned rather hostile to the new Chief Minister. In a small state like Haryana, these measures work very well, and work fast; so, Ch. Bhajan Lal soon became a heavy weight compared to his rivals.

Professor Sher Singh was one of those who had returned to the Congress fold as a member of Ch. Bhajan Lal's band of forty. While Pandit Bhagwat Dayal Sharma, a Governor appointed by the Janata Party in 1977, had continued in his position, Professor Sher Singh, after crossing over to the Congress camp, had once again become a Minister at the Centre. Ch. Bansi Lal, much maligned and humiliated after his party's and his personal defeat in 1977, had adopted the policy of lying low. Thus, Ch. Bhajan Lal was quite comfortable so far as the political challenge from his rivals within his own party and from the opponents in the other parties was concerned.

Ch. Devi Lal's own camp was in disarray, nor was he the sole master of the state unit of the Lok Dal, since the party was headed at the national level by Ch. Charan Singh who, though dependent on Ch. Devi Lal in the state of Haryana, did not have much liking for his unbridled ways of acting unilaterally in his own little territory. In other words, the internal tension of the Lok Dal was cause enough for satisfaction to the ruling Ch. Bhajan Lal.

The only danger to Ch. Bhajan Lal's position in Haryana politics could come from the unrelenting hostility of the Jat community. Usurpation of the state power from the Jat leader, Ch. Devi Lal, by someone from a community not even known in most parts of the state, except the district of Hisar, was considered something of a deep dishonour, almost a public shame, by the dominant community. The Jats were waiting for the moment of revenge, forgiveness having no place in their political behaviour.

Besides, the Punjabis, largely committed to the ideology of the RSS, would vote for the Congress Party only when the Party of their own liking, the BJP, was not in a position to get into the seat of power. As for the middle and lower castes, while most middle castes owning lands had a natural inclination towards Ch. Devi Lal's party, known for its rural bias, the lower castes, traditionally the vote-bank of the Congress, were not always in a position to demonstrate their power equal to their numerical strength. By persuasion or by pressure, by money or by muscle, a sizeable portion of this vote-bank could be diverted to the opposition by the dominant caste of the Jats. With the passage of time, however, the lower castes have found their own force, no longer amenable to undue pressures.

In short, Ch. Bhajan Lal, during this short span of two years, as a convert Congress Chief Minister, did not feel sure of his victory in the next election to the state Assembly due in 1982. His hopes rested on the internal disharmony in the Lok Dal and his hold on the state administrative machinery, which he knew how to use to his advantage. Thus, the scales between the two camps of Ch. Bhajan Lal and Ch. Devi Lal were evenly balanced so far as the prospect of forming the govt. after the election of 1982 was concerned. Although not considered by Ch. Bhajan Lal as a very serious challenge, the Jat leaders within the Congress Party, the original Congressmen, such as Ch. Bansi

Lal, Ch. Birender Singh, and Ch. Samsher Singh Surjewala, could not be taken for granted. All of these leaders were ambitious, and as loyal soldiers of the party, they thought they had a more legitimate claim to the top position than the new convert Ch. Bhajan Lal.

Although he had described his joining the Congress Party as a 'home coming', Ch. Bhajan Lal's detractors within the Congress Party called it rank opportunism, not ready to trust him as a loyal member of the Congress. All in all, there was an air of uncertainty on either side, though the Lok Dal enjoyed a measure of sympathy on account of the humiliation Ch. Devi Lal, the leader of the Lok Dal, had received from those that snatched the reigns of power from him. The people of Haryana were keeping their fingers crossed, remaining uncertain about the electoral outcome.

Ch. Bansi Lal's period of lying low was over by 1982, and he had started entertaining the dream of staging a come-back as Chief Minister of Haryana. His son, Ch. Surinder Singh, meanwhile, had grown into a force of some political consequence. As President of the Youth Congress of Haryana, he had gathered quite an army of followers. His followers were an aggressive lot, ready to take tough measures on the slightest signal from their boss. Similarly, Ch. Samsher Singh Surjewala, on the strength of his seniority in the party, had earned a secure and strong position for himself.

Having as his political heritage the following of those committed to the politics of Ch. Chhotu Ram, whose daughter's son he is, Ch. Birender Singh was also emerging as a leader in his own right. So, if Ch. Devi Lal had his own worries in the Lok Dal, Ch. Bhajan Lal was not entirely free from those worries inside his own camp. All in all, the outcome of the coming election of 1982 could not be an easy guess for anyone given to making political predictions. Even the political pundits, the habitual fortune tellers, were rather perplexed.

When the election did come in 1982, Ch. Devi Lal seemed to have an edge, owing to the support of the Jat voters in the villages. But there is always the silent majority that keeps its cards close to the chest. Similarly, Ch. Bhajan Lal seemed to have the blessings of the Congress High Command to continue as the state Chief Minister in case the party was returned to power. In fact, that was the agreement struck with the Congress High Command when he did the political feat of converting his entire flock to the new faith. Political ambitions among politicians, however, cannot be set at rest by any sympathy or support available to the rival.

From beginning to end of the election process, moves and counter-moves were set afoot by all the contenders in the political arena of power, each trying to extract the maximum advantage for himself, creating the utmost impediments for the others. The players in the 1982 Haryana election were quite adept in the game of sabotaging, so dear to them. While Ch. Bhajan Lal, Ch. Bansi Lal, Ch. Birender Singh and Ch. Surjewala cherished the ambition to head the state government on the Congress side, Ch. Devi Lal and Dr Sarup Singh, wittingly or otherwise, had set up a rivalry of sorts between them on the Lok Dal side.

In the first round of the battle for the tickets, while Ch. Bhajan Lal succeeded, as expected, in cornering the largest share in the Congress Party, Ch. Devi Lal outwitted his rival, Dr. Sarup singh, in securing an overwhelming number of his followers contesting on the Lok Dal ticket in the election arena.

The battle lines drawn, the two potential leaders likely to head the state government, Ch. Bhajan Lal and Ch. Devi Lal, went about in their distinct styles of electioneering, with Ch. Devi Lal activating his aggressive supporters, mostly Jats, and Ch. Bhajan Lal supporting the candidates expected to win, both belonging to his own party as well as independents, with the necessary means for the victory. In fact, he lent invisible support to some in the rival camps as well, those that he knew could be won over if the situation so demanded.

In bourgeois politics, helping your own men to win is not enough; equally important is to help defeat those in the opposite camp, including the rivals in your own party. Both Ch. Devi Lal and Ch. Bhajan Lal being seasoned politicians knew this game very well, more than anyone else knew in the state of Haryana of their time. One of the weapons used in this game full of risks is to put up independents against those you wish to be defeated. And there is no dearth of formidable candidates in most constituencies for playing the spoil sport.

There are those who have been denied tickets by their own parties. There are also those who are rich and influential but having no position in any political party for managing the party symbol to contest election. Also, there are those who enjoy reputation and popularity among people but are unable to afford the ever-increasing expenses of elections. Whatever be the category, the aspirant for heading the state government has to lend solid support to the spoil-sports so that they emerge serious contenders, running alongside those considered the front-runners. Even if these spoil-sports do not win, they do ruin the chances of others. And if they do win, still better for the sponsoring leaders.

In terms of money in the year 1982, Ch. Bhajan Lal had a clear edge over Ch. Devi Lal; while Ch. Bhajan Lal had been Chief Minister for three years and had acquired large resources, Ch. Devi Lal, even though he remained Chief Minister for two years and had a much longer career in politics than Ch. Bhajan Lal, besides being a big landlord, was no match to his rival in the field of creating resources. Also, those with stakes in the government–businessmen, bureaucrats, technocrats–send support uninvited for anyone likely to win the election.

These clever classes invest in all those individuals and parties having some standing in politics, but those expected to win, individuals as well as parties, get the lion's share. Since Ch. Bhajan Lal was contesting from a position of power, still occupying the Chief Minister's chair, in receiving monetary support from sundry sources he had a clear edge over Ch. Devi Lal. Muscles may have bveen more powerful on the Lok Dal side, but money had a greater flow on the side of the Congress Party.

The outcome of the election results was a hung Assembly; no single party having a clear majority of 46 members in a House of 90. The single largest party was the Congress with 34, followed by the Lok Dal with 31. Ch. Bhajan Lal knew the importance of the single largest party, so he had made sure that he got more than his rival's band, majority or no majority. The rest, he knew, he was capable enough to manage. But the job was not as simple as it seemed. The Lok Dal and the BJP had contested the election in some sort of alliance, though with no common manifesto. So the two parties quickly combined to stake claim for forming the government. Grabbing the independents was the next job on hand, so both the groups got busy with the business. Some were easy catches, others rather tricky. One tricky case the author himself experienced, which is worthy of narration.

Since the author was also one of those who had been successful in the electoral contest, defeating from the constituency of Rohat in Sonepat district the Education Minister in the outgoing Cabinet of Ch. Bhajan Lal – Smt. Shanti Rathee – he was assigned the job of enlisting the support of the lone independent member elected from my district. Ch. Devi Lal had asked him to contact Ch. Rajinder Singh Malik, who was an old hand at the game. This gentleman was unique in that he preferred to get elected as an independent member. His philosophy was that since he could serve his constituency better if he became a Minister, he must be free to join the party that fomed the government. Becoming a Minister could not be a certainty in the bourgeois system even if your position in the party was among the seniors.

Ch. Rajinder Singh Malik knew it well, so he always prefered to contest as an independent; for whoever would form the government would do so with the help of experienced hands like him. It worked very well for him because for quite a while there was no single party securing a comfortable majority. Besides, there are always the inconvenient ones within your own fold who would not let you live in peace. Therefore, it is better that those not convenient are kept out of the Cabinet. The independents are the best friends, having no heavy demands for their groups as they have none. Hence the successful stint of Ch. Rajinder Singh Malik in Haryana politics. He became a Minister several times.

The reason why Ch. Rajinder Singh Malik succeeded in winning several elections to the state Assembly was his large following among the voters of his constituency. His philosophy was that those who support you must be helped at all costs, whether their demands are right or wrong, legal or illegal, moral or immoral. He would go all out to help his men, men who supported him in the elections. As a result, he had created a large, committed following for himself. In his constituency, parties were not of much consequence, personalities were.

Of course, the philosophy that Ch. Rajinder Singh Malik followed created an equal number of detractors as well. The reason was that whoever he helped he did so at the cost of someone else, and that someone else would turn his enemy. In rural constituencies like that of Ch. Rajinder Singh Malik, favours that your followers seek always relate to some feud with their neighbours. Now, to help one party in a feud means to invite the animosity of the other. Ch. Rajinder Singh Malik did not mind enemies so long as he made friends among voters.

So it was this gentleman, Ch. Rajinder Singh Malik, whom the author was expected to win over to the Lok Dal side, to help form a government headed by Ch. Devi Lal., though the writer was not well-versed in the art of winning MLA's. He was rather naïve by temprament as well as by training. Besides, he knew little about Haryana politics, certainly not about the kind of politics the leading players in the game had created over the years. We know how in the very first election to the Haryana State Assembly, in 1967, our legislators had earned a name for themselves all over the country.

Aya Ram, Gaya Ram still remains a label reserved for Haryana legislators, although it is losing its sheen now since the introduction of the Anti-Defection Act, making crossing over to the other side almost impossible. The condition of two-third majority for changing sides is against the very temper of a Haryanvi. Freedom loving as they are, they have never felt at home in organizations of all sorts, especially the type the CPI or the CPM prefer to have, imposing a strict discipline of staying within the bounds of the code laid down for its members.

The point is that the author being the wrong person for the subtle art of seeking the support of a freedom-loving individual legislator of Haryana, the mission was bound to fail. And so it did. Ch. Rajinder Singh Malik and the writer, living in the same town of Sonepat, with no direct clash of interest, had a formal regard for each other. So Mr. Malik welcomed the writer as his younger brother and asked him what had brought him to his door. When the writer broached the subject to him, his simple condition was that he would not take a second to lend support to Ch. Devi Lal if he could show him 45 on his side.

Well, how and where it should he done, the author had no idea. Mr. Malik was right on his side, for he would not take the risk of joining a side that would not succeed in the game of numbers. Forty six members were required in an Assembly of 90 to form a govt., and he as an individual could only be 46th; he would not like to be 45th or 44th, that being a risky step. The author appreciated his position and went back happy as the man assigned to him for manipulation had not said no, and was willing to join if the Lok Dal managed to collect the required number. But by the time the author could reach where Ch. Devi Lal was, to give him the positive news, Ch. Rajinder Singh Malik had already joined Ch. Bhajan Lal's band. He was quite senior, and a seanoned one at that. How could he make a mistake?

At the same time, Ch. Devi Lal, along with Dr Mangal Sein of the BJP, had managed the required number of 46 to stake claim for forming the government. The author thought of Ch. Rajinder Singh Malik and felt that his friend had for once made a mistake, of not joining the winning side. So the claim was staked. All the 46 went to the Raj Bhawan, where Sh. G.D. Tapase, the then Governor of Haryana, welcomed the flock with all courtesies, and finally, feeling satisfied with the claim, fixed Monday, which was two days later, as the date for the swearing-in ceremony. Ch. Devi Lal and his flock returned jubilant, with the crowds waiting outside Raj Bhawan bursting with joy, making the city roads quite a sight. The citizens of Chandigarh soon saw the spectacle of rural Haryana spread all over, leaving no room for the smooth flow of traffic.

All the 46 of Ch. Devi Lal's flock were housed in the neighbouring state of Himachal, in a hotel of the state's tourism corporation. This was at Parvanoo, which begins where Kalka, the last town of Haryana, ends; the two are so close to each other that but for the barrier at the border one would not know where the one ended and the other began. Well, the non-Congress camp at once got down to distributing sweets among themselves, surrounded by a swarm of supporters who revel in such occasions. The harder ones took to drinking beer or whiskey, leaving the softer ones to sweets.

Ch. Devi Lal, being the leader, had not forgotten the task ahead. He asked the author to sit with Ch. Virender Singh, a close confidant of the leader, known for his shrewdness, and prepare a list of those who would be presented to the Governor for swearing in as members of Ch. Devi Lal's Cabinet. Dr Mangal Sein was, of course, to be consulted, being the leader of an alliance partner. As the exercise of drawing up the list of would-be ministers had just got underway, there came a flash news on the radio–there was no television then–that Ch. Bhajan Lal had been sworn in as the next Chief Minister of Haryana.

The news was a rude shock to all those at Parvanoo, but most so to Ch. Devi Lal who, after a long struggle in politics spreading over 50 years, had been denied his due, his legitimate claim to the seat of power to rule Haryana. He was in a boiling rage, with his eyes red, his fists clenched. Those with him feared that he would physically take on some one, most probably the Governor who had done him wrong, a grave injustice. His men knew he was capable of acting physically– something all simple and honest men do when their moral sense is outraged. Ch. Devi Lal had earlier attempted such an act, at least once, as a senior political leader. One incident relates to 1965, when the division of Punjab was being considered by the Commission appointed for the purpose. Another relates to the time of the Emergency when he had slapped a senior Congress leader in jail.

The first incident deserves a description. Calling one by one the leaders from the Haryana region, who were Ministers in Punjab or at the Centre, including important legislators and Members of Parliament, the Commission ascertained their views on the proposal to create the state of Haryana. While Professor Sher Singh and Ch. Devi Lal made a strong plea for the creation of Haryana, Ch. Ranbir Singh and Ch. Bansi Lal thought it wise to leave the matter to the discretion of the central leadership. Ch. Bansi Lal is, in fact, said to have remarked that there was no need for a separate state of Haryana because small as it would be, the govt. of the new state would not be able to afford even the salary bill of its serving cadres.

When Ch. Devi Lal came to know of Ch. Bansi Lal's position, he rushed to the latter's residence, got the news confirmed, and took out his shoe, the longest that a man may wear, and tried to hit the traitor. Ch. Bansi Lal was smart enough to sense his senior's mood right at his arrival, so he at once took to his heels just when Ch. Devi Lal had stretched his hand for his shoe. Professor Sher Singh was a witness to this drama of sorts.

Thus, knowing what Ch. Devi Lal was capable of, his juniors tried to placate his anger. Ch. Virender Singh, Dr Mangal Sein and the author collected the flock of 46 and went into a meeting, seriously considering the next step to combat the sudden situation created by the unethical, and perhaps unconstitutional, action of the Governor in making Ch. Bhajan Lal the Chief Minister of Haryana. The Lok Dal-BJP camp decided to march to Raj Bhawan the very next morning. And they did that at the appointed time. Ch. Devi Lal paraded his men, all the 46, to the the press and the public, exposing the fraud the Governor had played on the Constitution.

But in the murky politics of our time, nothing much happened to the world beyond Haryana, and even within Haryana the reaction remained mixed, there being an equal number of supporters on the other side as well. But Ch. Devi Lal remained true to himself : He reached out for the chin of the Governor, while sitting face to face, although Ch. Virender Singh and the author had flanked him on either side to ward off the expected action of indiscretion on the part of their leader. His hand was strong and long enough to do what he had decided. He did touch the Governor's chin; the incident was blown out of proportion by a section of the press, reporting that the Governor was 'slapped' or 'man-handled'.

Such shows of resentment as Ch. Devi Lal had made may enlist public sympathy, but they do not upset the political applecart, based as it is on hard decisions, the ones that remain untouched by soft matters like the people's sympathy. So Ch. Bhajan Lal's taking over as the Chief Minister of Haryana had become a hard reality. What remained was only a lingering hope of proving the majority on the floor of the House to be summoned within a month of the swearing-in-ceremony. One way to meet the challenge was to take the entire flock outside of Haryana and lodge them in a non-Congress governed state, as the BJP has been doing of late. This was suggested to Ch. Devi Lal, the leader.

But like any other hero of tragedy, Ch. Devi Lal had a tragic flaw: he would forget the seat of power, if offered the temptation of addressing the masses. So a grand rally was organized at Chandigarh to expose the foul play the Governor had indulged in at the behest of the Central government in Delhi to deprive Ch. Devi Lal of his legitimate claim to form the government in Haryana. Ch. Devi Lal at once forgot his flock as also the necessity of keeping them in safe custody: He took to his favourite recourse of reaching out to the people and seeking their support.

The case of Ch. Devi Lal in relation to the masses reminds us of Dr. Johnson's remark about Shakespeare in relation to quibble. Both had irresistible attraction for their respective weaknesses. Suitably substituting Ch. Devi Lal for Shakespeare and 'masses' for 'quibble', the Johnson passage on Shakespeare would aptly describe the force that drove Ch. Devi Lal to political disasters (or glory in his own ethics). The changed text would read as under:

> The masses were to Ch. Devi Lal, what luminous vapours are to the traveler; he followed them at all adventures; they were sure to lead him out of his way, and sure to engulf him in the mire. They had some malignant power over his mind, as their fascinations were irresistible. ...The masses were the golden apple for which he would always turn aside from his career, or stoop from his elevation. The masses, poor and barren as they are, gave him such delight, that he was content to see them, by the sacrifice of reason, propriety and truth. The masses were to him the fatal Cleopatra for whom he lost the world, and was content to lose it. (Desai, 107)

So, Ch. Devi Lal lost the crown and the castle, so to say, and forgot it all as soon as he saw the sea of people spread over the vast lawns of the City Beautiful (as Chandigarh is called). While he was absorbed in his address to the masses–his style of speech was to avoid oratory and turn the speech into a sort of dialogue with the masses–a number of clever guys slipped away and made a long journey to Delhi and got in touch with the man of the moment, who had acquired by then the reputation of the master craftsman of Haryana politics, who pulled legislators to his side as the magnet attracts iron files.

By the time the band of Ch. Devi Lal's legislators reached Delhi at the Ranjit Hotel in Rouse Avenue quite a few had departed to their expected abode. Two cases are worth the mention here. One is of Lala Brij Mohan Singla, who had been elected from the urban constituency of Jind. When the defeated flock got up next morning at the Ranjit Hotel, the newspapers had carried the front-page story, reporting that a Haryana legislator had escaped from the hotel by climbing down a drain pipe. After a long day's journey with three or four public meetings addressed by Ch. Devi Lal on the way from Chandigarh to Delhi the legislators were sleeping like logs, knowing not what had happened in the mysterious night of the murky city.

These ruralites of Haryana in a Delhi posh hotel were no better than the poor quadrupeds housed in a zoo. One good thing about a rural character is that in times of stress he would rather have a joke than worry his head with problems. These legislators of the Lok Dal had hearty laughs imagining how Singla must have made it down the drain pipe. It fired their fantasy and they churned out a hundred tales out of the event or incident. Only Ch. Devi Lal and his son were a little worried, although they had almost got used to worrying rather easily by now after all they had lost between Delhi and Chandigarh.

The second case is that of Col. Ram Singh Yadav, elected at that time from the urban constituency of Rewari. When Ch. Devi Lal chose to stop at Sonepat to address yet another public gathering, Col. Ram Singh Yadav had convinced him that two MLA's – Ch. Lal Singh and Ch. Azmat Khan – were likely to escape. In order that they may be prevented from doing so, counselled the clever Colonel, it would be safe to leave them to his custody. Ch. Devi Lal readily agreed, so naïve was he among the set of smart guys who were to manage the future politics of the state. Providing safe custody to the two low-profile legislators, the Colonel took them to Haryana Bhawan in Delhi.

The first thing Colonel Ram Singh Yadav did on reaching there was to deposit the two precious catches in his room and get in touch with Ch. Bhajan Lal. The latter welcomed the Colonel and admired his skills in bringing to his fold two more, besides himself. Colonel Ram Singh Yadav knew how to strike a political deal to his advantage, and so he did, but not without some rewards to his poor appendages as well – like an aristocrat, he was known those days for his generous ways in his dealings with his colleagues. He became the Speaker of the Haryana Assembly, which he found rather dull.

Thus, with a few more adventurers crossing over to the cosy camp of Ch. Bhajan Lal's ruling outfit, his controversial government easily won the trust vote and got into the saddle, distributing *laddoos* to all and sundry, hanging outside the state Assembly or loitering around the Chief Minister's residence. The jubilation was, of course, in a low key, keeping in view the circumstances in which the entire game plan was prepared, guarded, and executed. Soon after his political success, Ch. Bhajan Lal, never a cheat in the fair game of politics, rewarded all those who had stood by him in the hour of trial, including those who had deserted their own sinking boat, only to lend support to the sailing ship.

Distributing befitting prizes to these men of softer metal, who had walked all the way from across the fence, to lend support to a leader in need, Ch. Bhajan Lal expressed his heart-felt thanks to them, saying that they had set before the people of Haryana an example of ideal political conduct. True to his word, Ch. Bhajan Lal made them ministers, and handed over to them keys of their official cars as well as of their allotted houses. All's well that ends well! So was it for Ch. Bhajan Lal and his men.

Thus, Ch. Bhajan Lal's short maiden innings as the Chief Minister of Haryana, though it had come about as a coup, led to the next full innings of five years, forcing Ch. Devil Lal and his men to undergo a sort of follow-on. If it was the weapon of coup that had made Ch. Bhajan Lal the Chief Minsiter of Haryana in 1979, it was the still more subtle weapon of outmanoeuvring that carried him to the cushion the second time. Having more political armours in his store than available to the simpler leaders like Ch. Devi Lal, Ch. Bhajan Lal always felt confident that he could defeat his rival at will on the new turf of state politics. Decidedly, the elder statesman belonged to the old world. No wonder Ch. Bajan Lal had started declaring himself a Ph.D in politics, dubbing his opponents as only Highschool novices in the game.

7

Ch. Bhajan Lal's Full Term 1982-1987

The double defeat of Ch. Devi Lal at the hands of Ch. Bhajan Lal was rather too much to swallow for the Jats; they became doubly unfriendly to the latter. In keeping with the law of nature, following its functioning of action and reaction being equal and opposite, Ch. Bhajan Lal saw his political survival in showing a clear preference in all matters for his now well-defined constituency of the non-Jats. The Brahmans and the Punjabis and the rest became his favourites in bureaucracy, in police, in lower cadres, in further recruitments, etc. This clear tilt sharpened the political divide between the Jats and the non-Jats.

In a way, this suited Ch. Devi Lal also, for his following became all the more staunch and unshakeable without his doing anything substancial in return for his followers. In fact, the Jat–non-Jat antagonism suited the two leaders so well that gradually they came to work in tandem in crucial moments; they sounded at times as if they had made Haryana politics a bicycle with seats and pedals for two riders, one behind the other, or a carriage drawn by two animals harnessed one in front of the other.

The way Haryana politics developed in those years, between 1979 and 1999, Ch. Devi lal and Ch. Bhajan Lal seemed to hand over the reigns of power to each other as if the two were working in a rotation system. Recently, at a public rally in the constituency of Ch. Bhajan Lal, when the present Chief Minister, Ch. Bhupinder Singh Hooda, made a stinging remark saying, "the politics of match fixing, which has been going on for long, would not work any longer," his point was to draw attention to this very phenomenon of rotation between the two Lals. Since it went on for a long while, quite a few in politics started believing in the suspicion that somewhere beneath the surface there was an undeclared understanding between the two.

The conjecture may or may not be true, but the fact remains that in politics there are no permanent friends or enemies; it is only the exigency of a situation that will decide which combination would work. Winning or succeeding being the only goal in politics, it hardly matters who you are required to embrace and who to attack. This fundamental principle of bourgeois politics is true of all the players in the game, not just of Ch. Bhajan Lal and Ch. Devi Lal.

Whatever be the case, in 1982, when Ch. Bhajan Lal managed to become for the second time the Chief Minister of Haryana, the task cut out before him was very clear: he had to keep his varied flock of legislators humoured, and he had to cater to his constituency of the non-Jats. And so he did, seldom failing to see his targets or to hit them. The legislators were made more than happy; they could not have asked for more. As for the constituency, that too was well-fed on the illusion that the government of Ch. Bhajan Lal was their own government.

People in a bourgeois democracy, we know, have to sustain themselves on illusions. Their problems, we also know, will remain where they have always been; they only look for some sweet dream to sleep with, some intoxicant to get over the pain and keep going. The sentiment of fraternity, of feeling one with your own casteman, whenever one gains a little prominence in politics, in services, or in sports, is a reflection of that illusion or opium. The illusion one gets is that now it is all yours; the man there is your own man, and now all will be well.

Ch. Bhajan Lal and other politicians know the power of this illusion very well, and they take full advantage of the potency of an illusion, which is a very effective, efficient, and inexpensive agency. One needs only to oblige an individual of a community, any individual convenient and pliable, obedient and serviceable. And there is no dearth of this species of the human race; they are there in plenty in all castes and communities. And yet the castes and communities live in perpetual antagonisms, despite there being such a common species among them, despite there being such a common attraction for the illusion. It may be a sort of cynicism, but one has to accept that the great Manu understood human nature a little too well. The castes in our country have proved it for centuries. Whatever the growth in science and technology, sociology and psychology, we have maintained the dividing lines of castes at all costs; no cost is high enough, not even our lives, when it is a question of protecting the honour, the identity or the interest of our caste.

Our desperate search for discovering our own gods and kings, the symbols of our solidarity and vanity, each caste for itself, is only an expression of that firm commitment on our part to the purity and sanctity of our own castes. We raise the statues of our gods and kings, our great castemen, and we worship them. At the same time, we hold our hard-earned democracy dear; and yet we hold our kings, and our gods, dearer. This reverence for the icons of caste and community, and that illusion of nominalism as universalism, of taking the welfare of any of your castemen as your own, as the community's own, has a common ground; both function on the same principle and follow the same logic. Our caste affinities continue to be tribal, though our aspirations are going global.

Returning to the immediate and the actual, Ch. Bhajan Lal used the principle of nominalism quite effectively. He not only gave jobs to individuals of the supporting communities, but also created statues and study chairs for the kings and gods of different castes and communities. Ch. Bhajan Lal created in the process an image for himself, an image of a soft and sweet person, no man's enemy, ready to oblige one and all, suggesting to all the easier way of life. Whenever he found that a Minister or an officer had not requested him for a favour, he himself would call such individuals and offer them a petrol pump, a gas agency, or a discretionary plot. This earned him a great reputation among these privileged people. 'How caring, how good and great the Chief Minister is'; they would always remark. 'Great' indeed he always is whenever in office, more so whenever out of office. Politicians in general are the sweetest and most hospitable, when they are out of power.

In our blessed state of Haryana, though, deeply shocking things also keep happening, irrespective of who is holding the reins of power. Hard to drop from one's memory are the murders of two women, one at Hisar, and the other at Yamuna Nagar, which took place in the 1980's. In Hisar, there was a school teacher named Sushila, who made the mistake of preventing the wards of certain so-called V.I.P.'s, some petty politicians, from copying in the examination. The woman was abducted, taken to different places for two months, gang-raped as and when the gangmen desired, insulted and humiliated by the ruffians, and finally killed in cold blood. In the city of Hisar, people know who these boys are, and their names did figure in the newspapers. The rogues are said to have escaped the punishment they deserved. 'The way of the world', one remarked. Aren't such things happening with greater frequency today than ever before, and as many in Hayrna as in other states of our motherland?

The other murder was no less henious. At Yamunanagar, a gril named Renuka was one day returning from school. She happened to reside close to someone's shop, where one of the shopkeeper's friends, a close relation of a so-called V.I.P., was a frequent visitor. This scoundrel on seeing the girl demanded her possession, which the shopkeeper arranged by telling her a lie that her parents had left the key at his place. As soon as the girl entered the shopkeeper's place, she was gagged, taken inside, gangraped, killed, and her body bundled into a *bori,* which was found on the railway track. In this case also, people in Yamuna Nagar know about those involved, but again the rogues remain unpunished. The privileges of poiliticians are plenty, unless of course one runs into the territory of someone enjoying greater privileges than one's own.

These days, such cases have become quite common, and people's response indifferent as to a routine happening. They read so many cases of the kind reported, and skip over to the next page, and after going through other pages, put the newspaper aside. What else can common people do? The police is in the service of the privileged, not the people. Even witnesses dare not come forth, for it is they, rather than the criminals, who would face harassment in the police station, and then in the courts. All for what ? For justice, which is never in sight to a common man. He would better spend his time more fruitfully earning his bread by doing whatever labour is in store for him.

The Chief Minister, whoever he may be, would, directly or indirectly, willingly or unwillingly, be found to extend protection to the privileged, for it is this class of people, the MLA's, the M.P.'s, and their relations, financers, supporters, who, after all, keep his government going. The common masses will be taken care of at the election time. The VIP's will press all their manpower as well as their money power in shielding their kith and kin. Besides, people always vote for whoever seems ahead of others, in whose favour the wind seems to be blowing. That wind can be created by community leaders and caste heads, who are not a difficult lot like the unruly masses, for what they require is only respectable and honourable treatment, with, of course, a little more to live comfortably. All this is not a big deal for the seasoned players in the game of politics. They have grown among these elders; they have dealt with these elders; and they have known inside-out these figures of straw. The rogues that rule the roost roam like wild beasts, untamed by the agents of law, prowling for their prey, the underprivileged poor.

Such murders are, of course, a routine matter for the administration, which will go on as they have always gone on. In any case, they have no bearing on the game called power politics. So, we better get back to our main story, narrating some more important events involving the rulers of the state. In the period of Ch. Bhajan Lal's term beginning 1982, the problem of Sikh militancy had come up. There was nothing abrupt about it though, for the assassination of Smt. Indira Gandhi in 1984 was itself an index to what was in store for the years to come, even as it was a climactic event of the militant crusade for Khalistan.

This tragic event had taken place because she as the Prime Minister of India had felt duty-bound to check militancy in Punjab, which was apparently inspired by forces across the border in Pakistan. No Prime Minister could have compromised on the integrity of the nation, which the leader of the militants, Sant Jarnail Singh Bhindranwala, had threatened. The event was, in fact, climactic in the turbulent history of the time. The demand for a separate Sikh state, independent of India, recognized by the United Nations, was not acceptable to the Govt. of India, nor to the people as a whole, not even to more than half the population of Punjab itself. But the movement had come up like a fire in the settlement, which neither Ch. Bhajan Lal nor those at the Centre could afford to ignore.

Since many protests and rallies were being organized in Delhi by the Sikh bodies, including the Shiromani Akali Dal headed by S. Gurcharan Singh Tohra and S. Prakash Singh Badal, Ch. Bhajan Lal as the Chief Minister of Haryana – a state between Punjab and Delhi – had a role to play. He was expected by his superiors in Delhi to stop the entry of the Sikh volunteers into the capital city, Haryana being the buffer state between Delhi and Punjab. This brought into prominence the role of Haryana in national politics. There being both a sense of duty and a show of loyalty to the High Command of his own party, Ch. Bhajan Lal did the job in all seriousness, deploying unprecedented police force on the Punjab and Delhi borders.

Once the police gets such a job to do, we know what it is capable of. So, every Sikh became a target of search on the road to Delhi from Punjab. In a way, the police had no option either, for how would they know who is innocent and who not without stopping and searching every Sikh. And yet, S. Prakash Singh Badal, driving a truck, did manage to reach Delhi where he publically set fire to certain pages of the Constitution. But ordinary Sikhs felt humiliated and insulted, carrying a feeling of discrimination, which naturally comes more easily to those of the minority community than to those of the majority.

The end result of it all was the alienation of Ch. Bhajan Lal from the Sikh community, which has a sizeable presence in Haryana. He started receiving letters of threat to his life, making not only him but other Haryanvis also targets of attack by the terrorists. Several incidents of bomb blasts took place at Kurukshetra, Pehowa, Panipat, Ambala, etc., in which lots of people, innocent people, lost their lives. Not only that Ch. Bhajan Lal invited the wrath of the Sikhs, the Congress Party also got alienated from the Sikh voters.

The assassination of Smt. Indira Gandhi left behind such bitterness between the Sikhs and the Congress Party that despite apologies tendered first by Shri Rajiv Gandhi, who took over from his mother the office of the Prime Minister of India in 1984, then by Smt. Sonia Gandhi, who continues as President of the Party, the Sikhs have continued to remain hostile to the Congress in general and the Gandhi family in particular. It is only after Sardar Man Mohan Singh was made the Prime Minister of India in 2004 that the Sikhs have softened somewhat their hostility towards the family and the Party. This last event was an intelligent move by Smt. Sonia Gandhi for more reasons than one.

The most hurting incidents of that time were first the military action on Harminder Sahib in Amritsar to flush out the militants hiding in the shrine, and the aftermath of Smt. Indira Gandhi's assassination when several thousand Sikhs were burnt to death in Delhi, Haryana, and other places in the country, but more so in Delhi and Haryana. An inadvertent remark attributed to the young Prime Minister, Shri Rajiv Gandhi, made things still worse; the remark being, when a big tree falls, some tremors are bound to take place. It reflected a sort of royal temper one finds in a character like the wife of Julius Caesar who in Shakespeare's play with that title remarks:

> When beggars die, there are no comets seen.
> The heavens themselves blaze forth the death of princes.
> (Harrison, 826)

The remark, made by Shri Rajiv Gandhi, or mischievously attributed to him, acted like salt sprinkled on a wound; the Sikhs still carry the feeling of animosity towards the dead – we know Shri Rajiv Gandhi himself became a target of terrorist attack in 1991, though his killer was not a Sikh.

The fall out of all this on Haryana politics was that the Congress Party lost for a long while the sizeable support of the Sikhs in Haryana. This suited most the opposition leader in the state – Ch. Devi Lal. Right from the 1970's, or perhaps even earlier, Ch. Devi Lal had found in Sardar Parkash Singh Badal a strong political ally. Ever since Ch. Devi Lal left the Congress Party in 1968, when he was denied the party ticket, he had aligned himself with the Akali leader, the two families coming so close to each other that the strong tie between the two is still continuing, with the younger generations on either side acting in perfect coordination in both business and politics. Ch. Devi Lal, of course, knew no business, nor did Sardar Parkash Singh Badal; it is only the younger generation that has ventured into business and has done so with a vengeance, making up for the follies of their fathers.

The recourse to business by the two families was perhaps the call of the time, for by the 1980's, and more so in the 1990's, the politics of the country had become a big business. Those who did not have tons of money could not lead a party or form a government. Both based on the strong regional sentiments, the Lok Dal in Haryana, an exclusive concern of Ch. Devi Lal's family, and the Siromani Akali Dal in Punjab, solely managed by the Badal family, are not used to functioning within the framework of any larger political organization like that of a national party.

Ch. Devi Lal did merge his outfit in 1989 with the Janata Party, leading to the formation of the Janata Dal, a national party, though a short-term formation fated to split soon after. Even within the framework of the Janata Dal Ch. Devi Lal had maintained the Haryana unit as an independent outfit not accountable to any national leader or organization. The moment any leader or party ever attempted to interfere in his exclusive affair, Ch. Devi Lal would split that party and float an independent regional party. Whatever be Ch. Devi Lal's political party – the Congress, the Lok Dal, or the Janata Party – his alliance with the Akali leader, S. Parkash Singh Badal, always remained intact.

After 1984, Ch. Bhajan Lal's government in Haryana had more troubles in store. Soon after the events of 1984 were initiated, or relivened, the contentious issue of Chandigarh and the division of the river waters between Haryana and Punjab surfaced. This suited both the Lok Dal in Haryana and the Akali Dal in Punjab. In all probability, the issue was raked up by the two in close consultation with each other. But the plan for the struggle for their respective rights, mobilising the masses against the Congress rule in both the states, targeting the Assembly elections due in 1987, had to be suspended in view of the sudden declaration of the 1984 election to Parliament.

Although due in 1985, the Congress thought it expedient to cash on the sympathy wave in its favour after the assassination of Smt. Indira Gandhi. Ch. Bhajan Lal, too, found a task cut out for himself. One simple expectation, as from any Chief Minister, was that he should win for the party a maximum number of seats. With the wave already there in favour, the task was not difficult, the only worrying factor being the hostility of the Sikhs which could make a difference in the constituencies neighbouring Punjab, there being a sizeable population of the community in these constituencies.

The sympathy wave, however, was so strong that the Congress Party won all the ten seats in Haryana – a record of sorts, because ever since the creation of Haryana the Congress Party had never before bagged all the seats. Stalwarts like Ch. Devi Lal and Dr Sarup Singh were defeated by men either little known or known for wrong reasons. While Ch. Devi Lal was defeated by Ch. Dharam Pal Singh Malik, Dr Sarup Singh lost to Sant Hardwari Lal. Election time is also the best opportunity for any Chief Minister to get rid of his rivals. He does it on the principle of 'kill with kindness'.

The kindness is that he recommends his rivals as the best candidates for certain constituencies. The kill is that he gets rid of his rivals with a kind cut. If the rivals win the election, the Chief Minister takes credit for the right choice, conveniently sending his detractos out of the state. And if the rivals lose the election, so much the better, for that would ruin even their future prospects in state politics. Ch. Bhajan Lal played this game with Ch. Birender Singh and Ch. Samsher Singh Surjewala sending them both to Parliament in 1984, the former to the Lok Sabha, the latter to the Rajya Sabha.

The strategy is the same in all the parties, for the rules of the game called politics are standardized, grown classical owing to their long-standing credibility. On the Lok Dal side, Ch. Devi Lal had extended the same courtesy to Dr Sarup Singh who, in the state Assembly election of 1982, had appeared a rival, fearing that the latter would stake claim to leadership if the Lok Dal came out victorious in that election. The game was successful: Dr Sarup Singh lost the election to his rival Ch. Hardwari Lal. To his own dismay, Ch. Devi Lal also lost the election from Sonepat, losing it to a light weight, Ch. Dharam Pal Singh Malik. With this big loss it became all the more urgent for Ch. Devi Lal to raise some popular issue for ensuring his party's victory in the 1987 - election to the state Assembly.

Ch. Birender Singh may have taken to heart his ouster from the Haryana politics in 1984, but in the long run it proved a blessing in disguise. Although he did not get any Cabinet berth in Shri Rajiv Gandhi's government, he did get a chance to come close to the young leader, so close that by the time the next election was around the corner in 1987, the young Prime Minister had made up his mind to hand over the Party's Haryana leadership to Ch. Birender Singh.

What actually happened in 1987 and then in 1991 we shall take up later. But all that one wills or wishes, one plans and proposes does not necessarily take place. In fact, more often than not, it happens otherwise. As Shakespeare has observed:

> Our wills and fates do so contrary run
> That our devices still are overthrown;
> Our thoughts are ours, their ends none of our own.

So what we plan, plot, or conspire, may turn out to be contrary to our planning, plotting, or conspiring. Not only that, the contraries in life are so interwoven that good leads to bad, and bad to good, there being hardly any segregation between the two. But let us leave philosophy aside, for that is the last thing politics, especially the practical, will ever care to think of.

As an aftermath of the 1984 setback to the Lok Dal, power politics in Haryana soon hotted up. It seems quite natural, and also reasonable, that the defeated leaders should try to rise from the fall by raising a storm, smaller efforts being of no use in reaching from the earth to the ethereal heights. The other fallen stalwart, besides Ch. Devi Lal, was his friend in Punjab, Sardar Parkash Singh Badal. The two naturally combined to create or cook-up a common cause. And when these two combine, we can always expect a tough political challenge for the rival camp. Ch. Bhajan Lal had to bear the brunt from both sides. From behind in Punjab, Sardar Parkash Singh Badal raised dark clouds of the movement for Punjabi Suba, sponsored, supported, and spearheaded by different outfits in the land of the war heroes.

From the front, Ch. Devi Lal took up the issue of Chandigarh and Fazilka-Abohar in the land of greenery. Although the two were officially pitted against each other, being contenders for the disputed territory; under the ground, there was a collaboration and coordination, quite formidable for any government, hard to crush, harder still to avoid its adverse consequences. The Punjab challenge, aimed straight at the Union Govt. in Delhi, was only indirectly affecting the Congress government in Haryana. Since Haryana falls inbetween Punjab and Delhi, Ch. Bhajan Lal had to contend with agitators of all hues, who had to travel to Delhi to press for their demands, which ranged from retaining the disputed territory to the creation of a separate Sikh state.

On the home ground of Haryana, the defeated Lok Dal took to 'the patriotic' cause of the people of Haryana. A meeting of the party functionaries was called to chalk out the strategy for the long struggle. The author being the Chief Whip of the Lok Dal in the state Assembly and a General Secretary of the Party's state unit, also participated. It was decided that an agitation under the heading Naya Yudh be launched to secure justice for the people of Haryana, who had been discriminated against by denying them the city of Chandigarh, despite its being awarded to Haryana by the Shah Commission appointed to propose linguistic division of the earlier Punjab state.

Later, in Smt. Indira Gandhi's time, Fazilka and Abohar areas were awarded to Haryana by another Commission in lieu of Chandigarh. Even the second Commission's award was not implemented because of the strong opposition from the people of Punjab. Although Prof. Sher Singh and Ch. Devi Lal tried on all occasions to create a matching pressure from Haryana to counter the threatening postures from Punjab, the former could never really raise the kind of fearful situation the Akalis and their official and unofficial allies did in Punjab.

Right or wrong, for good or for bad, Punjab has been feared by the successive governments at the Centre, whereas Haryana has always been treated lightly, considered no serious threat to the law and order of the land. The popular images of a Punjabi and that of a Haryanvi are viewed as antithetical: while the former is considered aggressive, ready to die if needed, the latter is taken as humble, not very self-conscious about his religious or regional identity.

By nature, a Haryanvi is perhaps peace-loving, law-abiding, and contented to live in local conditions. However, life in Haryana is fast changing now, with rising unemployment and global economic pressures, resulting in a rapid increase in violence and a tendency to move out of the mother country. All this goes against the grain of the traditional Haryanvi. Two examples that come to mind would reveal some truth about the archetypal Haryanvi character.

One revealing instance is the case of the Hindi agitation in the mid-fiftees of the last century, headed by Professor Sher Singh, against the condition of compulsory knowledge of Punjabi for all those seeking government jobs in Punjab – Haryana in that period was the Hindi-speaking region of Punjab. Prof. Sher Singh, the Deputy Chief Miniter in the Cabinet of Sardar Partap Singh Kairon, had resigned not only from his position in the Govt. but also from the Congress Party, and had given a call to the people to rise against the unjust imposition of a language not their own. About thirty thousand people went to jails, and remained there for several months.

When finally the agitators were released, a Rohtaki remarked, addressing the leader Professor Sher Singh, "I am not going to join in future any such agitation that lands me in jail, even if your *Hindgi* (for Hindi) dies crying for support." The metamorphosis of Hindi as a cow in the remark reveals the vital imagery the Haryanvi dialect so naturally uses. But more important is the total unfamiliarity of the man making the remark with the hazards of an agitation. He had never thought that it could also mean lauguishing in jail for months or years. The man here can be taken as a representative of the Haryana people in general, showing how they love placidity and calm, rather than seek martyrdom through agitations, especially of a radical nature, for causes not of particular interest to them.

Another instance relates to the author's tenure as legislator from 1982 to 1987. An important assignment of an M.L.A's work in Haryana is the transfer of government employees, over ninety percent of whom are school teachers. Mostly, the school teachers in Haryana are posted in their own districts. The requests these teachers bring to you every year is to transfer them to either their own respective villages or so close to them that they can conveniently commute on their two wheelers between home and school. The question always is: How close? The effort goes on for years until you are right in your own village school.

One such example is unique. A school teacher, whose transfer the author could not manage, being an M.L.A. in the opposition, requested that the author should get him suspended. It surprised the author, also offended him. But for enlightenment, the author asked him why he wanted such a fantastic help from him. His reply was that suspension would be revoked sooner or later and he would get the arears of his salary, but this would make it possible for him to look after his business of fisheries in his own village where he was earlier posted.

Now, compare these Haryanvis with those in Punjab who would go out anywhere on earth to seek better fortunes. No wonder they are in every place known to the civilized world, and perhaps even in places not quite familiar to the civilized world. The border states or regions in most countries generally develop the outgoing, adventurous spirit, whereas those living in the interior continue to remain inward-looking, contented in a closed world. The Haryanvis are known for the culture of the interior.

The Punjabis are known to be pushing in life, doing business, driving taxis in New York, or whatever; the Haryanvis are known for their inhibitive quietness, too much attached to the native land. The Punjabi teachers, even if they have to supplement their incomes from salary by doing some side-business, would find better ways than seeking suspension to stay home.

An education report of the Union Ministry of Education in the 1980's admits the practice of proxy teachers, more prevalent in Punjab than in any other state, where a permanent teacher sublets his teaching to an unemployed graduate on a paltry sum of a few hundred rupees, even as low as Rs 200 per month, and himself devotes his time to do his side business.

The two instances, thus, reveal the vital difference in the two cultures, although the two regions have been parts of a common province or state of India for a long time. Popular perceptions are, of course, seldom based on hard facts. The historians have their own explanations for this difference, so have the sociologists. Leaving it for them to theorize and to substantiate their theories, we better get back to Haryana politics as it was developing in the mid-1980's.

The *Naya Yudh* planned by the Lok Dal headed by Ch. Devi Lal in Haryana was to take off with rallies and *rasta roko,* finally to descend on Delhi with large *jathas* of people starting their march to Delhi on foot from different places in the state. Rallies turned out to be terrors for the town shopkeepers. In one of the rallies at Rohtak the crowd went out of control resulting in looting of shops and manhandling of those who tried to resist the plundering rowdies. Police had to be pressed into action to restore law and order in the town.

Luckily, no one got killed in the firing to which the police had to resort when the rowdies were not heeding any warning nor fearing any mild action like the *lathi*-charge. But what followed is interesting. A leader (the author would not name), on being told what had happened, at once asked, "how many were killed in the police action?" When he was told 'none', one could see grave disappointment on his face. "Had even one been killed," he said, "our agitation would have got the boost, leading to crowning success."

Well, in politics, nothing is of no use, and the least usable is the most useful. A scene from John Steinbeck's novel *In Dubious Battle* comes to mind. When a worker in action among his comrades on strike gets killed in police firing, the workers gather to mourn his death forgetting that they have to continue their struggle at all costs. When their leader, Mac, finds them down with grief on the loss of a comrade, he firmly speaks to them the following:

> We've got to take him, I tell you. We've got to use him to step our guys up, to keep'em together. This'll stick them together, this'll make'em fight. (Steinbeck, 121)

A soft and sentimental worker, Dakin, not quite conversant with the struggle of the working class, calls Mac and Jim (another leader) "cold-blooded swine" who "think of nothing but 'strike'."

Well, that's how things go in a war, any kind of war – strike, agitation, or fight ! The *Naya Yudh* we were in was no different. In the next stage of the struggle, *rasta roko,* we met with greater success. The best way to stop traffic on roads, it was decided, was to fell trees readily available on either side of the road. Since this illegal step of felling trees was not quite acceptable to some of the legislators, they were given the option of adopting some less objectionable mode of protest. So, some of them managed to make do by just squatting on the road in a *dharna*. These Lok Dal men were removed by the police after a few hours, and they cooperated when they were taken into buses to a police station nearby where they were let off. This was on the Grand Trunk Road. Th police, too, turns friendly if the agitating party is a prospective winner in the election around the corner.

On the country routes in the interior, things were altogether different. Those in command, or unable to command, found their followers, after felling trees, indulging in more serious unlawful activities, like burning vehicles. As a result, firing took place at some trouble spots, resulting in three deaths. The inevitable had finally happened, by design or by accident. It set the whole state 'on fire,' so to say. The rural folk, more so the Jats, the vocal activists of the Lok Dal, were furious. They were now ready to go to the extreme to take revenge upon the "anti-people" government of Ch. Bhajan Lal.

After the desired success of the second stage (*rasta roko*), the Lok Dal was in high spirits; the party's following had grown manifold. Now, any call for action against the government would be a success. So, the third stage, of marching to Delhi, was at once planned and put into effect. *Jathas* were formed, each headed by an M.L.A. – there were over twenty to lead these *jathas*. All *jathas* began their march the same day and were to culminate at Delhi after a week or ten days. Arrangements were made on the way for night halts and routine meals on time. This proved a successful way of involving large numbers of masses in the movement for the crucial cause of the state. The long journey spread over seven days or so was not dull; there were interesting things happening; also, entertainment of songs, dances, skits, etc., was a part of the programme that had been well thought-out and put into effect. One incident that the author still remembers, being most interesting, is not without significance either.

The night halts of the *jatha* included drinking as an item of the evening meal. Of course, not all members were given to drinking, but quite a few were. While the workers spent their nights in the camps organized for the purpose, the author always reached his home in Sonepat for the night stay. In a way, he was unable to 'mix up' with them the way they easily mixed up with each other. Also, if he had stayed with them in the same camp, they would not have the freedom to abandon themselves in drinking, abusing, etc. So, the arrangement suited not only the author, but equally the party workers.

Once late in the night – it was past midnight – a jeep stopped at the author's door and he heard the door bell ringing. So, he went out to know what the matter was. It was a group of three or four from the *Jatha* with an emergency situation on their hands. The author was told that after the usual evening drinks, which generally went on till late in the night, two of them got into a brawl. Before the two could be separated, one of them had bitten away one of the ears of the other. He was found holding it in his mouth, which he later spat out on the ground.

This company of three or four were carrying in a piece of cloth that unlucky ear. The author at once went with them to the camp, took the injured man with him in the jeep, and reached the small town a few miles away from the camp. The doctor was kind enough to readily stitch the separated year in its rightful place. It, of course, took months before the victim recovered from the injury. The man who had caused that injury was totally unaware that not long after he would emerge a leader of sorts in the state politics, exercising quite an influence, and carrying a committed following in a small segment of the state, quite firmly his own. Strange, they say, are the ways of destiny. You never know what is in store for you. This young man was no wiser about his future.

The rally at the *Lal Quila* (Red Fort) grounds in Delhi was really grand, perhaps unprecedented. People descended from all around Delhi as also from the far-flung areas of Haryana, swarming and spilling over the grounds, spreading far beyond the Ring Road, making a sea of humanity. Ch. Devi Lal had it in him : he could attract large crowds by giving a call for a cause. He was, indeed, a mass leader. Haryana has not had any leader of his stature after Ch. Chhotu Ram.

Ch. Chhotu Ram, of course, had similar appeal. But the author was only six years of age when he died and did not have the benefit of seeing his public gatherings. Haryana, at that time was, a part of united Punjab, which included not only the present-day Haryana, Himachal, and Punjab, but also what is now called East Punjab – a major chunk of Pakistan, and the dominant one. So, Ch. Chhotu Ram had a much larger sphere of influence than that of Ch. Devi Lal. Both were mass leaders in the real sense of the term. Others have been in power, and for longer periods than either Ch. Chhotu Ram or Ch. Devi Lal, but none with the mass following these two enjoyed. Their following was, of course, not without the tinge of the caste: Both remained in public perception 'Jat leaders'.

To return to the Lok Dal's Naya Yudh : As it became more and more threatening, more and more the people felt sure that Ch. Devi Lal's party would win the next election. The prospect of the Lok Dal capturing power in Hayrna sent the panic signal to the Congress High Command in Delhi. Ch. Bhajan Lal, as usual, tried to put up a brave face, although he was deeply shaken within. He tried hard to convince the High Command of his party being equal to any challenge and there was no cause for worry. But the worry kept on gaining a deeper hue. What came out of the worry would form the matter of the next chapter. So, let us close the present one.

8

Ch. Bansi Lal as Night Watchman 1986-1987

Ch. Bhajan Lal's Govt. was getting panicky, faced as it was from both sides with powerful challenges. On the one hand, Ch. Devi Lal was getting aggressive, on the other, Sardar Parkash Singh Badal was turning radical. The Punjab leader's demonstrations in Delhi could be successful only if he succeeded in pushing large numbers of his followers through Haryana. On the home turf of Haryana, the followers of Ch. Devi Lal were getting more and more aggressive, eager to force an early election. The last great rally as part of the *Nayaya Yudh* agitation was held at Jind, which was even larger than the one at Delhi.

The much smaller town of Jind than the city of Delhi found itself taken over by a mass of rallyists, their vehicles, and their abandon. It sounded a warning to the central command of the Congress Party. In a fit of panic, the party went for a change of guard. Ch. Bhajan Lal was replaced by Ch. Bansi Lal. In a way, they changed places: while one left the central ministership and became the Chief Minister, the other left the Chief Ministership and became the central minister. The role of Ch. Bansi Lal was like that of a night watchman in cricket sent to hold on until the day's play is over. Here, in this case, the expectations were much more than normally expected of a watchman; Ch. Bansi Lal was also expected to go on to perform a long innings to win the 1987 election and ensure for himself a full term of five years.

This change of guard in Haryana in 1986, just one year before elections to the state Assembly due in 1987, once again revealed the unideological and caste-oriented politics of the Congress Party. Ch. Bansi Lal being a Jat, the Party thought he would be able to reduce the influence of Ch. Devi Lal in the community. Also known for his high-handed style of functioning, it was expected of him that he would subdue the rising aggressiveness of the Lok Dal voters.

Another factor that perhaps favoured Ch. Bansi Lal was that he was known to be a 'doer,' a man who could deliver the goods, showing developmental results in the state. But once the people make up their mind to change a government, nothing works, much less mathematical calculations of caste considerations or personality predilections. The people of Haryana had made up their mind, and nothing could avert their verdict, which any one could read on the great wall of popular perception.

An aspect of the Congress Party's political philosophy, highly practical, is to go for the majority community, give it the top post of the Chief Minister, as also the impression that it had the natural right to rule, being the majority caste or community. The Party has been practicing this politics in whichever state it has had the chance to form the government. In Jamu-Kashmir, the Muslims are the privileged community; in Punjab, the Sikhs, more so the Jat Sikhs; in Himachal, the Rajputs; in Haryana, the Jats. And this, despite the fact that the results of this philosophy have been disastrous. The roots of militancy both in Jamu-Kashmir as well as Punjab can be traced to this philosophy.

But does the Congress Party, or, for that matter, any other party replacing it, have any choice in the matter ? Perhaps not, for the states of the Indian Union were created on a linguistic basis, and the smaller circle of that language-speaking mass gives the majority an easier ground to dominate than would be allowed by a multilingual mass in a wider circle. Decidedly, the smaller the territory, call it a state, the easier for a caste or community to dominate the minorities.

No wonder the agitations for a separate state both in Punjab and Haryana were not only spear-headed but started and sustained respectively by the Jat-Sikhs and the Jats. In Punjab, the Hindus were dead opposed to the idea, and perhaps rightly, for they knew what they were in for. In Haryana, the non-Jat castes and communities were not opposed to the idea, but they were not enthusiastic either and remained almost aloof from the movement, whatever that movement was. The fact that the Akalis launched, spearheaded, and sustained the agitation for a separate state on the Punjab side, and the Jats headed by Ch. Devi Lal and Professor Sher Singh produced a semblance of agitation on the Haryana side, would require no deep analysis to know the motivation behind their efforts.

The hard fact about Indian politics, however, is that except for the Left parties – CPM, CPI, RSP, F.B., etc. – no other political party is wholly free from the taint of casteism or communalism. The Congress, compared to the other bourgeois parties, certainly emerges more secular and modern than any other. It is these 'worse' parties that give the Congress an advantage in Parliament, although the situation is not the same in the state Assemblies.

As already stated, the linguistic basis of our states, not unrelated to caste and community clusterings in the various parts of our country, weakens in every state the dominance of the national parties, more so the secular ones. It is for this very reason that the Congress Party has lost many states to the regional or communal parties. Right from the days of the princely states, and perhaps from even the earlier times, Indian society has been ruled by caste and community leaders. Our kings were caste or community leaders who continue to remain the symbols of identity for every caste and community. So, let us leave the matter at that and return to our small state, and its smaller politics, being caste based, and wholly free from the burden of ideologies which remain as alien as Greek to an average Haryanvi.

As the election to the state Assembly came still closer, Ch. Bansi Lal as Chief Minister worked hard to recover the lost ground. At about the time he took over the reigns of power in the state, the author was spearheading an agitation of farmers demanding non-realization of the cost from them for the RCC lining of the water canals in the state. The author had to lead the agitation because the first arrest of a defaulting farmer had been made in his constituency of Rohat (Sonepat). The Govt. plea was that since the work was completed with the loan drawn from the World Bank, the user farmers were to pay the cost. The farmers' plea was that much more is spent by the Govt. to promote industry in the state. Why not extend the same soft treatment to the poor farmers that is being given to the rich industrialists?

Trying to win over the farmers at the election time, Ch. Bansi Lal acceded to the farmers' demand and thus partly succeeded in softening the farmers' attitude towards the government. Another good thing that happened in 1986 for Ch. Bansi Lal was the split in the Lok Dal, not only in the Haryana unit, but also in the Bihar and U.P. units, involving in the forefront of the rebellion that led to the split leaders like Shri. Ram Bilas Paswan, Dr Sarup Singh, Thakur Rameshwar Singh, Ch. Rajinder Singh, and Dr. Bhim Singh Dahiya, all of whom were expelled from the party for "anti-party" activities.

The Lok Dal split begged a few questions: Firstly, was it all to challenge the autocratic style of functioning of the state chieftans, such as Ch. Devi Lal in Haryana, Shri Karpoori Thakur in Bihar, and Shri Mulayam Singh in U.P.? Secondly, was it a game plan on the part of some master-players, such as Shri Chander Shekhar, the then president of the Janata Party? Thirdly, was it all a manipulation on the part of the friends of Ch. Bansi Lal? Lastly, was it a routine step of the Congress Party, the ruling party at the time, to allure a few disgruntled elements to break away from the rival party at the time?

All these questions are related to each other, and perhaps none can be ruled out, if all these factors are studied in detail and in depth. There were the detractors of the Lok Dal's state chieftans; there were the friends of Ch. Bansi Lal; there were those inimical to Ch. Devi Lal and friendly to Ch. Bansi Lal; and there were the parties that would welcome a split in the rival camp, others that would welcome additions to their own ranks. Not all of those in the rebel camp were aware of the actual cause that rocked the Lok Dal ship. Some of them later realized that perhaps they had been used in the game by the smart and seasoned ones.

Some less and some more, but all of these factors seem to have worked towards the common target of causing a split in the Lok Dal. Donations from 'supporting' individuals or business firms also seem to have played a vital role in bringing about the split in the Lok Dal. On the face of it, the event seemed an important one, with a bunch of stalwarts walking out or pushed out of a political party. The timing of the event was considered significant, and aroused suspicions on both sides. All this happened on the eve of the election – just about one year before the election to the Haryana Assembly held in mid–June, 1987. All of those who left the Lok Dal were not quite aware of the machinations behind the event. But all are not expected to know the secrets of poilitics. Only the leaders enjoy that privilege. But what seemed to sound a big jolt proved at last a small pinch – something that had no effect whatsoever on the outcome of the election.

However, these seeming shots in Ch. Bansi Lal's arm proved of no avail before the storm that Ch. Devi Lal and his men had raised with their hard work over the years – the storm also had as one of the igniting fuels the grouse the Jats and the majority of rural masses still carried against Ch. Bhajan Lal who had deprived Ch. Devi Lal twice of his due. That hurt had not been healed. But the hurt was perhaps not as powerful as the tempting promises Ch. Devi Lal had made to the people. It was these irrisitible promises that swelled many –fold the electoral support to the Lok Dal, swelled by the non-Jat farming communities that otherwise kept distance from the Jats. He had declared that all the loans of the farmers would be waived off within a week of his assuming power in the state.

Another attractive promise carrying mass appeal was that old age pension would be given to one and all after the age of sixty. These promises worked wonders, with the entire mass of people itching to have the voting date at the earliest. And when the day of reckoning came in 1987, people gave the combination of the Lok Dal and the BJP headed by Ch. Devi Lal the unprecedented majority of 85 out of 90 seats in the state Assembly.

One may wonder what ensured the majority in such a measure. It may be the Jat community's anger against Ch. Bhajan Lal and its sympathy for Ch. Devi Lal – anger against the former because he had deprived the latter twice of what seemed his due; sympathy for the latter because he had been robbed of his political earnings. Believe it or not, the people of Haryana, especially the Jats, are a strange lot; they have in ample measure both anger and pity. When in anger, they can show the crudest form of cruelty. We daily read instances of a husband chopping off his wife's head with a spade, or a son shooting his father, so on and so forth.

As for pity, one instance would explain it all. Ch. Dharam Pal Singh Malik of Gohana lost several elections in a row between 1996 and 2004, the reason being his unpopularity among the people for his failure to come upto their expectations when he was in power for twelve years between 1984 and 1996. When the Haryana Assembly Election of 2005 was held, people at once decided to elect him, because, most would say, he had lost for a number of times. In fact, the moment the said election was declared, the people of Gohana constituency had made up their mind even before the candidates had approached them for votes. The reason was 'pity'; they felt he had received enough punishment in the form of several consequtive defeats. In another case, someone in jail accused of murder was voted to the legislative membership just out of pity – a sympathy wave worked for him. The Haryanvis may not be credited with morals of a refined society, they certainly possess strong passions of a primitive society.

One can also attribute, as stated earlier, Ch. Devi Lal's astounding success in 1987 to the tempting slogans he had raised, promising on oath to implement them on assuming power. This was, decidedly, a strong, if not the sole, reason for his success. Anger, pity, and temptation, all played their parts, in small or in great measure. What seems to have been the least possible reason for the electoral success was the Haryana-Punjab inter-state dispute about territory and water. It seems we humans are more interested in personal, contingent, and urgent interests, than in the general issues of state or nation, region or community.

Also, the contesting parties both in Haryana as well as Punjab have never been frantically committed to issues like Chandigarh or the river water. They do have their prestige attached to these matters, but there has never been any urgency after they had secured their separate states. These larger issues are always kept in reserve for the election time. They come in handy whenever the election is declared, but they are as quickly forgotten thereafter as they are raised.

Not only the Akali Dal and the Lok Dal use these issues as election slogans, the Congress and other parties do the same whenever the occasion so demands. Perhaps the general public on both sides is not as guillible as the leaders take them to be. Their considerations, too, are different from these abstract issues. The decisive election issues, after the initial heat following the bifurcation of Punjab in 1966, have always been other than those of Chandigarh and the river water.

A classic instance of this political device is the issue of *Mandir* at the *Ram Janam Bhoomi* in U.P. The BJP has used this issue every time the election is declared in U.P., as also in some other states, in the last twenty years. The issue was framed by the party in the 1970's. The author remembers once a friend with strong RSS roots had told in 1978 how their cadres would carry a brick each from every village in the country, walking to the *Ram Janam Bhoomi* site in U.P. When the author commented that from the plan explained to him, it seemed, the task to be completed would take a few decades, his reply was that it was not his party's plan to raise the temple in the near future.

On asking why then undertake the gigantic exercise of launching a hundred-year long war, he said the real purpose was to mobilize mass support for the party. The cat was out of the bag. But why blame the BJP ? All the bourgeois parties look for catchy slogans at the election time, never meaning to put them into practice. At long last, the BJP seems to have realised that any issue raised too many times loses the heat and becomes dead. In the last Parliament election held in 2005, the issue was not raised at all.

Of late, political parties in India have gone the American way. They engage advertising firms to design slogans and other publicity material for them, and they spend huge amounts of funds on advertising. In this age of media dominance, everything gets sold through advertisements. In fact, 'out of sight, out of mind' works well in our time. If you can't afford to display your products, that too repeatedly and aggressively, you will not be able to survive more than a few seasons. As the big companies are putting the small companies out of business, so the moneyed families in politics are finishing off aspiring individuals, disabling them from the electoral contest.

No wonder the only agenda the contesting individuals and parties have is to expand their business of politics in order to become more competitive. A simple comparison of the legislators of our time with those of yester years would show the big change that has taken place. Politicians like Ch. Chhotu Ram, Ch. Tika Ram, Ch. Lehri Singh, Prof. Sher Singh, Pandit Sri Ram Sharma, etc., are hard to find in this age of commerce. These people, even after a life-time in politics, did not have enough possessions of their own. Some of them had no car of their own, and could be seen moving about in rickshaws when not holding a Cabinet position. Most of them did not even have houses of their own in the big cities where they lived.

One of the realities of Haryana politics, amply illustrated by the election of 1987, is that the Congress has been the single strong political party in the state, its main stay being the scheduled castes and backward classes, whose total strength counts for more than fifty percent of the state's population. The other major political parties in the state – the Lok Dal, under different variations of its nomenclature, and the BJP (earlier Jan Sangh) – have come to power only when the two have contested the election in alliance with each other. The last time in 2005, the BJP decided against an alliance with the Lok Dal headed by Ch. Om Parkash Chautala.The result was that they fell short of the majority, conceding it to the Congress. The BJP's argument was that its partner only takes advantage of the alliance for capturing power, and thereafter ill-treats the junior ally. The two, it is quite apparent from their cultures and ideologies, have nothing much in common with each other except their antagonism to the Congress.

The Lok Dal and the BJP constitute the antagonism of the rural and the urban, the peasantry and the trading class. And yet both had to be bed-fellows, however strange, every time the election came, forgetting the acrimonies of the five years between them. After all, who would not put up with discomforts and distastes to enjoy the bed of roses, the joys of power. The two shared it in 1967, then in 1977, and then in 1987. Their turn, obviously, came every ten years, and generally did not last the full five–year term. In 1967, it worked for less than one year; in 1977, for two years; in 1987, it remained good for four years. The Congress has always been ruling alone, and mostly for the full term of five years.

To return to the 1987-election, the turbulent period of the Congress party ended in peace, losing the complete ground to the rival combine of the Lok Dal-BJP. The Congress Party and its state leaders found themselves in the silence of the grave, with nothing to contend for, except the ruling combine's strength of eighty five in the House, and the indifferent crowds in the field outside. At home, in its own camp, there was hardly any activity, stunned as the party was by the most humiliating defeat it ever experienced in the state of Haryana.

The Congress Party's defeat in Haryana became all the more humiliating because of the party's ignominous situation in the face of the Bofors scandal, directly related to the party's leader, Shri Rajiv Gandhi. Although he was later cleared of the charge, that came about after several years of embarrassment the party had to live through, including the loss of the next Parliament election in 1989.

So, at such a time as 1987, Ch. Bansi Lal and his partymen had no choice but to keep a low profile and look after their individual domestic affairs. And they did just that, and for the long period of four years. Between 1987 and 1990 the Congress Party had nothing in store for it except repeated defeats in the elections to both the state Assembly and the national Parliament. Hard times for the Congress which had ruled the country and most of its states unchallenged for several decades.

9

Ch. Devi Lal and His Proxies 1987-1991

There has been a saying in Haryana that whereas Ch. Bansi Lal was the lion when in power, Ch. Devi Lal was the elephant in the field. You reverse the order and you see the reverse side of their personalities. Ch. Bansi Lal out of power would prefer to remain in hiding, and Ch. Devi Lal in power wouldn't know what to do with himself. In other words, while Ch. Devi Lal was a man of the masses, not quite comfortable in office, but at his best in the field, leading the people to a rally; Ch. Bansi Lal was most effective in office, a ruthless administrator, but not quite comfortable in the field, having no rapport with the people.

Once again, Ch. Devi Lal proved it: his ineffective performance as administrator. He could manage men in the field, but not legislators in the House, nor officers in the secretariat. With eighty-five legislators to satisfy, Ch. Devi Lal had quite a task in 1987. He made some of them ministers, some chairmen of Boards and Corporations. But, after all, how many could he really accommodate in these plum posts?

The problem with our legislators is that they have absolutely no interest in the business of legislation. Their only interest is in making full use of their privileged position to become powerful persons. All this interest is outside the House, in the field where the voters are, where the wealth is, where the privileges are. Therefore, the Chief Minister's job is to provide them with enough outside the house, with so much that they develop stakes which they would not like to lose at any cost. But that required a man altogether different from the kind of man Ch. Devi Lal was.

Between 1977 and 1987, Ch. Devi Lal's eldest son, Ch. Om Parkash Chautala, had grown to be a powerful force in the family as well as in the party, sidelining at the home front his two younger brothers who entertained ambitions of sharing power with him, and subdueing in the party all those who thought they had claims to at least assist Ch. Devi Lal in the task of governance. Very soon, even the most senior among them, like Ch. Virender Singh, came to realise, that their very existence in the Cabinet position as well as in the party depended on the goodwill of this man, the man behind the throne, the eldest son, who had firmly got into the back-seat and started managing the drive his own way.

This time around, in 1987, one could see that a new type of politics was emerging, as also a new kind of leadership. The values Ch. Devi Lal had stood for, the values of personal honesty and social commitment, were beginning to look outmoded, or otherworldly. Now, what mattered most was one's success by all means, success in the election, and success in the governance, whatever the means one adopted to keep going. Values of the corporate world were beginning to replace those of the partriarchal society. Ch. Devi Lal's old-world values looked old fashioned.

Ch. Devi Lal in his populist style completed two years, fulfilling the promises he had made to the people. The aged started getting old-age pension, and the farmers' loans were waived off. Both these measures were of great social and political significance. Personally, too, Ch. Devi Lal gained genuine goodwill of a large section of society. He became still taller among the masses. But then came the election to Parliament in 1989. The Bofors scandal made the non-Congress parties see a chance in the changed climate. They started striking alliances to form a stronger force to challenge the Congress.

The Janata Party and the Lok Dal decided to merge. A convention was called at Banglore of the leading members of the two parties. The author too, along with friends like Shri Ram Bilas Paswan, attended the convention. Shri Chander Sekhar was elected the President of the new party named Janata Dal. History seemed to repeat itself. In 1977, too, Sh. Chander Sekhar was elected to head the newly formed party. With the example before them of 1977, most of those at the convention hoped the Congress would once again be defeated, and the non-Congress parties would get a chance to rule the country.

What had been desired and expected came true: The Janata Dal in alliance with several other parties formed the Government at the Centre, with Shri V.P. Singh as the Prime Minister and Ch. Devi Lal as the Deputy Prime Minister of India. In fact, at the meeting of the M.P.'s called to choose the leader, it was proposed that Ch. Devi Lal should be asked to head the new government. But he showed the rare gesture of declining the offer, proposing instead the name of Shri V.P. Singh for the top position.

Ch. Devi Lal's decision to take up national responsibilities was bound to affect the political situation in Haryana. The fact that between 1989 and 1991, within the short span of two years, Ch. Om Parkash Chautala took oath as Chief Minister three times, and was made to step down every time, respectively after days, weeks, and months, indicated the growing impatience of the next generation to replace the old. But the fact that Ch. Om Parkash Chautala had to make way for nonentities like Master Hukam Singh, or for an old horse, like Master Banarsi Dass Gupta, also showed that the heir apparant (Ch. Om Parkash Chautala) had not yet emerged as the undisputed leader of the party.

The merger of 1989 had brought into the Lok Dal fold several persons who were averse to the leadership of Ch. Om Parkash Chautala. The merger created a mixture of disparate elements hard to homogenize into a cohesive compound. No wonder the government fell one year before the completion of its term of five years. The fact that six or seven oaths of office were administered in four years once again proved the Lok Dal's deficiencies as a ruling party.

The older generation in the Congress Party, too, was getting a little unsure of its grip, was afraid of losing power to one of the younger leaders eager to grab the much awaited position to lead the party. Ch. Birender Singh, like Ch. Om Parkash Chautala, was getting impatient. He had got an opportunity to come close to Shri Rajiv Gandhi after becoming an M.P. in 1984. His ouster from state politics, so cleverly managed by Ch. Bhajan Lal, had, in fact, proved a blessing in disguise for him. Well in advance of the Assembly election of 1991, Sh. Rajiv Gandhi had decided that if the Congress Party came to power, the latter would be made the Chief Minister of Haryana. Ch. Samsher Singh Surjewala, too, was an aspirant, who at the time was the President of the state unit of the Congress Party. But the young leader heading the national organization, Shri Rajiv Gandhi, had thought of Ch. Birender Singh as the fit person for the state Chief Ministership.

That the wishes of Sh. Rajiv Gandhi and the ambition of Ch. Birender Singh were not to be fulfilled is another matter, for the course the events take in life cannot be determined in advance by any individual or organization. As Shakespeare in one of his plays, *Hamlet*, has said,

> There's a divinity that shapes our ends
> Rough hew them how we will. (Harrison, 929)

It will be seen how the human wishes come to naught, the events taking an unprecedented turn at the election time, proving the pertinence of Shakespeare's observation, so relevant to actual experience, call it destiny if you will.

Ch. Birender Singh was given an upper hand in the distribution of tickets for the Assembly election of 1991. Ch. Bhajan Lal was not even made a member of the State Committee that was to recommend the names to the High Command for the 90 Assembly Constituencies. The author saw how he went from person to person in Delhi, to those considered close to the party president, and yet Sh. Arjun Singh, the man incharge of the task in hand, would not allow him entry into the room where the meeting was being held to decide upon the names of probable candidates. The author happened to be there at Sh. Arjun Singh's residence and saw Ch. Bhajan Lal sitting in the waiting-room attached to Shri Arjun Singh's office at his residence, waiting for the signal that never came. The author accompanied him to Shri M.L. Fotedar's house, but even that visit did not work.

On the other side, in Ch. Devi Lal's camp, the younger brother of Ch. Om Parkash Chautala, Ch. Ranjit Singh, who had been made a minister in 1987, along with some of his friends like Master Ran Singh Maan, Shri Kirpa Ram Punia, and Ch. Virender Singh, was trying hard to prevent his elder brother from capturing power in the state between 1989 and 1991. Every time the elder brother took oath as Chief Minister, the younger brother saw him deposed. This had happened three times. Once after a few days, the next time after a few weeks, and the third time after a few months.

Later, of course, the elder brother, the man with greater wits and undaunted perseverance, would see all these detractors out of the Lok Dal, converting the organization into his personal band of followers with unbending loyalty to him and him alone. Only his two sons would be allowed some share in the management of the party and administration of the state. That was to become possible a term later, the immediate one going in favour of the Congress Party.

Even at the worst of times in 1987, when Ch. Devi Lal had moved to Delhi as Deputy Prime Minister, vacating his Chief Minister's post as well as the Legislator's Constituency of Meham, Ch. Om Parkash Chautala did not lose his nerve, and managed to get control of things, though not without jerks and jolts given by the younger brother, Ch. Ranjit Singh. When the by-election to the constituency of Meham was to be held, he had managed to be nominated as the Lok Dal candidate, enjoying the blessings of his father who had always thought of him as his rightful and skillful successor.

The election event in Meham was no less than a battle, with both sides ready to go to any length. Violence followed, with workers fighting in the streets, the police compelled to take recourse to tough action, once even resorting to firing at the mob. The election ended with the death of a worker – on the side of the ruling party itself. The man who died was Ch. Amir Singh. All sorts of stories followed as to the cause of his death and the person(s) responsible for the same. No one seems to know the outcome of the court case that followed the death of Ch. Amir Singh.

The byelection ended, the race for Chief Ministership again started. Ch. Om Parkash Chautala by now had got hold of things in the party. After winning the byelection, he felt more emboldened. Even when he was prevented from taking oath as Chief Minister, he always succeeded in getting a man selected (elected) of his own choice. On one such occasion, a very simple, self-effacing, a habitual back-bencher, a loner, got into the seat, and continued for a few months as Chief Minister.

This man was Master Hukam Singh of Dadri (in Bhiwani district). With the tussle for succession on for about two years before the Lok Dal government finally fell in 1991, the affairs of the state remained utterly unattended. Besides, bickerings within the party and the government increased. The electorate certainly have no taste for infights in any party or government. It is the surest way of inviting defeat in the next election. And the Lok Dal did invite it in 1991.

Meanwhile, trouble had erupted at the Centre as well. Some thought, it had to, because, in their view, the government had to run into trouble if Ch. Devi Lal had anything to do with it, from inside or from outside. The fall of Shri Morarji Desai's government in 1979 was all due to him. Now, Sh. V.P. Singh's government in 1991 fell due to him. It all started with Sh. V.P. Singh's decision to implement the recommendations of the Mandal Commission, making 27% reservation in the central government jobs for the Other Backward Classes (OBC's). The decision had divided the ruling party and the Union Cabinet, with Ch. Devi Lal, Sh. Chander Sekhar, and their followers not in favour of the reservation. Whereas Sh. Chander Sekhar was in no position to do much beyond registering his own vote against it, Ch. Devi Lal had a government of his own in Haryana where things would happen the way he seemed inclined.

And so they did. A whole storm came up with a violent agitation in most Haryana towns, targetting the Central Government buildings, such as Post Offices, Railway Stations, Income Tax Offices, all of which were set on fire. Not that Ch. Devi Lal himself organized the agitation, but once his position became known to his followes, they raised a strom. The state government did do its duty in maintaing law and order, but despite the govt's best efforts, violence went on for months together.

The upheaval called the Mandal Agitation led to the fall of Sh. V.P. Singh's government. He was replaced by Sh. Chander Sekhar. Since the rebels had just about 50 members in a House of 542, the government was formed with the support of the Congress Party headed by Sh. Rajiv Gandhi. The German philosopher Hegel's famous saying, 'history repeats itself', once again came true. Just as Ch.Charan Singh had formed his government in 1979 with the help of the Congress Party headed by Smt. Indira Gandhi, so Sh. Chander Sekhar (another CS) formed his with the help of the same Congress Party headed by Sh. Rajiv Gandhi.

Interestingly, both Ch. Charan Singh and Shri Chander Sekhar were the same leaders who had respectively maligned Smt. Indira Gandhi and Sh. Rajiv Gandhi for their 'ignoble deeds' – Smt. Indira Gandhi for imposing Internal Emergency in the country, and Sh. Rajiv Gandhi for 'having a hand in the Bofors scandal'. Both these Congress leaders, mother and son, had played the politics befitting to the occasion. They supported their 'enemies' only to pull from under their feet the carpet at an appropriate time. Sh. Rajiv Gandhi did the same his mother had done. Sh. Chander Sekhar's government fell in 1991, and was made to face the election to Parliament soon after.

The 1991 election, in which during the campaign Sh. Rajiv Gandhi was assassinated, was held simultaneously both to Parliament as well as to the Haryana State Assembly. Historians have said a good deal on how and why the young leader, our former Prime Minister, was done to death, with an accusing finger raised on several persons in the power circle, the trail leading to the LTTE, whose several activists were arrested and brought to book after a long trial.

Our immediate concern being the politics of Haryana, we need to return to the events in the home state that showed fortune smiling on Ch. Bhajan Lal once again, and stunning Ch. Birender Singh who had received from his young master the assurance of forming the government in Haryana if the Congress Party was returned to power. To power the party was certainly returned, but the man who formed the government was not Ch. Briender Singh; it was Ch. Bhajan Lal who was blessed with the crown. How it happened, and why it happened, is an interesting story which must be narrated here in glimpses, if not in full.

Living in Delhi as a Member of Parliament between 1984 and 1989, and then later upto 1991, Ch. Birender Singh had developed a measure of closeness with Sh. Rajiv Gandhi, achieving some success in winning the latter's confidence. When the elections were declared in 1991, Ch. Birender Singh was given prominence in the state election committee that recommended candidates to the High Command for contesting the state Assembly election. As such, he was able to secure tickets for a large number of his followers, larger than those from Ch. Bhajan Lal's camp.

Sh. Rajiv Gandhi had made it clear to those of his aids incharge of the Haryana election that Ch. Birender Singh should be given the leadership of the state government in case the Congress came to power. With this undisclosed mandate from the High Command, Ch. Birender Singh got on to the high horse of hope and spread the High Command's message among his followers and those given the Congress ticket for contesting the election. If this helped Ch. Birender Singh in gaining assurance of support from the contesting candidates, it sent a warning signal to Ch. Bhajan Lal, who was determined not to miss the chance of getting another five years as Chief Minister.

Between 1986, when Ch. Bansi Lal had replaced Ch. Bhajan Lal as the Chief Minister of Haryana, and 1991, the time of the state Assembly election, Ch. Bhajan Lal had been in Delhi, first as Minister of Agriculture between 1986 and 1989, and then as M.P. between 1989 and 1991 during the non-Congress

Govts of Shri. V.P. Singh and Sh. Chander Sekhar. So, even if Ch. Bhajan Lal had not come as close to Sh. Rajiv Gandhi as Ch. Birender Singh, he was not located far away from the circle of power in Delhi. In fact, his ministerial residence in Delhi was next to that of Sh. Rajiv Gandhi as Prime Minister, which house he kept occupying right upto 1991. The author remembers visiting him during the election days of 1991 a number of times at that residence. In fact, it was from that very residence that Ch. Bhajan Lal's plans were hetched and executed for securing the Chief Ministership of Haryana once again.

Ch. Bhajan Lal, once aware of the move in the rival camp, became active as soon as the electioneering began. He immediately established contact with each candidate of the Congress Party, and with some even of the other parties, sending them material support from the very first week, increasing that support in the second week for those likely to win the race, finally overwhelming with his volunteer services all those who were sure to come out with flying colours.

Consequently, when the results came out, the number of winning Congress candidates was exactly the same that Ch. Bhajan Lal had predicted (51); his political arithmetic was never wrong. Ch. Birender Singh, too, approached all, those he thought were obliged to him for his help in securing for them his party's nominations. A large number of them were housed in the Haryana Bhawan in Delhi, with Sh. A.C. Chaudhary of Faridabad as their steward. Those wholly committed to Ch. Birender Singh were not required to be detained in the Haryana Bhawan. They were, in fact, let loose to secure the support of others from the rival camp.

Ch. Birender Singh was perhaps not sufficiently aware of the fact that his support-base had sunk the moment Sh. Rajiv

Gandhi was assassinated midway during the elections. The world had changed overnight, not only for Ch. Birender Singh, but even for the Gandhi family, later faced with the prospect of being pushed to the margin, even overboard, within the Congress party itself. Ch. Bhajan Lal being most flexible among the Haryana politicians had quickly made bridges with the new powers that were emerging at the Center. With Sh. Sita Ram Kesari as President of the Party and Sh. Narsimah Rao as the Party leader in Parliament heading the new government, Ch. Bhajan Lal had no difficulty in forming close equations with them; he only had to show his opposition to Ch. Birender Singh in Haryana and Sh. Arjun Singh at the Centre to prove his loyalty to the new masters; he soon established his credentials as 'their man'.

Ch. Bhajan Lal also knew certain other tricks of the game of politics unknown to Ch. Birender Singh. By the time the hour of reckoning came, he had secured the solid support of 43 MLA's out of 51, sparing for Ch. Birender Singh only seven (himself being the eighth). Goaded by the author's one–time antagonist, Ch. Hardwari Lal, he had assumed the role of a go-between to effect a compromise between Ch. Bhajan Lal and Ch. Birender Singh.

While on the one hand the author convinced Ch. Birender Singh that he had lost the game and the second best thing for him to do was to allow the unanimous election of Ch. Bhajan Lal, thereby getting the position of No 2 in the Cabinet, on the other the author persuaded Ch. Bhajan Lal to make a visit to Ch. Birender Singh's residence and make a formal request for his election as leader of the legislature party. Although both were hesitant in the beginning, they did agree to the proposal. Ch. Bhajan Lal did insist on meeting at a place other than Ch.

Birender Singh's residence, but the author explained to him how this would look graceful on his part, and he finally agreed.

The meeting was successful at the New Delhi residence of Ch. Birender Singh, near Rao Tula Ram Marg, where the author had waited for Ch. Bhajan Lal to arrive early morning (6 AM) to accompany him to the venue of the meeting, as he did not know its location. As had been agreed upon between the parties, Ch. Birender Singh assured Ch. Bhajan Lal that he would not contest the leadership election, and would, in fact, propose Ch. Bhajan Lal's name for leadership. Surprisingly, though, when the election meeting was held in Chandigarh the next day, Ch. Birender Singh forced the leadership contest and became the rival candidate to Ch. Bhajan Lal.

The author had to face embarrassment when Ch. Bhajan Lal told him about Ch. Birender Singh's breach of trust. It was more humiliating for Ch. Birender Singh as he got the support of only seven MLA's. Why he chose to break his promise and contest despite his full knowledge of the situation the author did not know, nor did he make any attempt to know it from Ch. Birender Singh. Dr. Ram Parkash, a senior office bearer of the Haryana Congress at that time, was his closest political friend those days. Some thought that Ch. Birender Singh was influenced by his friend.

All the same, Ch. Birender Singh did get a Cabinet berth, though his beta-noire, Ch. Samsher Singh Surjewala, got an upper hand by getting four more of his camp inducted in the Cabinet, which included Ch. Chhattar Pal Singh from the Ghirai constituency in Hisar, the young man who had given Ch. Devi Lal, the tallest leader in Haryana politics, a humiliating defeat in the election. Also included among the friends of Shri Surjewala was Ch. Tejinderpal Singh Maan of Karnal, who had won from the constituency of Pai. Another of these five was Ch. Nirmal Singh from the Nangal constituency of Ambala district, the young man risen from the ground on the strength of his own hard work among the people. Yet another new face in this Cabinet was Shri. Balbirpal Shah of Panipat, a Punjabi businessman who had also come up on the strength of his hard work among the people and in the party.

The election of 1991 gave a serious set–back to Ch. Bansi Lal in the Congress Party. In fact, it had become quite clear that the only option available to him after Ch. Bhajan Lal took over as Chief Minister, if he wanted to remain a political force in the state, was to quit the Congress Party and create his own outfit, however small. So he did! He and his followers (not many at the moment) floated a new political outfit called the Haryana Vikas Party. Backed by the business tycoon, Sh. Om Parkash Jindal, the new party found its feet in due time. As time passed, the Haryana Vikas Party started receiving the stalwarts from the Congress camp as well as from the Lok Dal.

On the other side, with Ch. Devi Lal defeated and his heir apparent, Ch. Om Parkash Chautala, not being among those elected to the Haryana Assembly from the Lok Dal, the mantle of leadership, though a sort of proxy, fell on Ch. Sampat Singh, a long-time loyalist of Ch. Devi Lal family. The number of MLA's on this side being not large, the opposition was not very effective, giving Ch. Bhajan Lal an easy time for ruling the state the way he liked. There was now also his elder son, Sh. Chander Mohan, elected from the Kalka constituency of Ambala district, to support him, even if unofficially. In fact, this time around, even the wife of Ch. Bhajan Lal, Smt. Jasma Devi, had started acting from behind the scenes and was able to influence his decisions as Chief Minister. Ch. Bhajan Lal's real strength now was, of course, the full-backing of the Center ruled by the Congress-led government of Shri Narisimah Rao.

Secure from all sides, Ch. Bhajan Lal got to rule the state for the first time with a free hand, there being no Nehru-Gandhi family at the Centre to nominate or disnominate anyone to the state leadership. The new Prime Minister being a dark horse for the posts he now occupied needed all the support from the states to consolidate his position as a new force in the Congress Party. Doing so was, of course, not an easy task, there being a strong lobby of the loyalists to keep the Party crown intact for the first family in Indian politics. Ch. Bhajan Lal being one of the most agile leaders in Indian politics soon got round the new centre of power in the Party and started calling the shots not only in Haryana but even at the Centre.

The next five years in Haryana politics would see the rise and fall in the fortunes of several stalwarts. Some would be shown the door, some others would find entry. All in all, as ever, the power politics of the state would continue to be colourful. Let us look into it then as curiously and as carefully as the events to unfold deserve! On to those events then that constitute the matter of the next chapter. The sooner, the better.

10

Ch. Bhajan Lal Once More 1991-1996

Ch. Bhajan Lal as Chief Minister remained unchallenged during the third term, as compared to his earlier tenures which were fraught with turmoil, there being on those occasions a lack of legitimacy to his taking over the reigns of power in the state. Both the times, in 1980 and 1982, he had been rather controversial, succeeding in forming the government more through manipulation than on popular support. This time, and perhaps the only time, he was there owing to popular support to his party, though not without snatching the support of MLA's from Ch. Birender Singh's camp. But that game is not uncommon or unusual in politics, and Ch. Bhajan Lal alone cannot be blamed for it. In fact, it was Ch. Birender Singh who proved unequal to his rival, and lost the battle for the top position, perhaps owing to his lack of political craft.

Ch. Bhajan lal was now so powerful that he could nominate the party president for the State Committee, raising Ch. Dharam

Pal Singh Malik to that position, whose wife the Chief Minister appointed as member of the Haryana Public Service Commission. Shri Malik was elected to Parliament in 1991 from the constituency of Sonepat, and gave a humiliating defeat to Ch. Devi Lal, the tallest leader in state politics. This double defeat of Ch. Devi Lal in 1991, losing in the Parliamentary Constituency of Sonepat as well as in the Assembly Constituency of Ghirai was the greatest set-back to the Jat leader, whose position among the Jats had been next only to Ch. Chhotu Ram. This shock defeat of Ch. Devi Lal was quite demoralizing for the party, leaving the workers in a state of disarray. The leader himself was not quite rattled; for, in his long career, remaining mostly in the opposition, he had got used to defeats and disappointments.

The Congress Party in Haryana had never had it so good ever since the formation of the state. At the Centre, too, some new stars had appeared on the horizon of Haryana politics. Besides Ch. Dharam Pal Singh Malik, who became the party president, Kumari Selja, the daughter of the late Ch. Dalbir Singh, a long-time Congressman, who rose to membership of the Union Cabinet and occupied that position for more than one term, became the Deputy Minister in Sh. Narsimah Rao's Cabinet, despite being a firs-timer to the Parliament. Later, during her very first term, she was made a Minister of State, although her department remained the same – Human Resource Development. Another new star on the horizon of Haryana politics was Rao Inderjit Singh, the elder son of Rao Birender Singh, a stalwart of Haryana politics who had become Chief Minister in 1967 by toppling the Govt. of Pandit Bhagwat Dayal Sharma. Rao Inderjit Singh also became a member of Rao's Cabinet as Minister of State.

Yet another star thrown up in Haryana politics was Ch. Randeep Singh Surjewala, the son of another stalwart in Haryana politics, Ch. Samsher Singh Surjewala, who has been winning elections to the State Assembly from the constituency of Narwana, and has also been a member of Parliament, and President of the state unit of the Congress Party. Ch. Randeep Singh Surjewala also created a sort of history by defeating Ch. Om Parkash Chautala from Narwana, from where his father had won several elections, and had nursed his constituency for more than one term as Irrigation and Power Minister. The duo of father and son continues to remain in the forefront of Haryana politics both being there in the present Assembly also (2005-2010).

The phenomenon of the rise of several sons (also daughters) around this time was, in fact, not new, neither to Haryana nor to other states of the Union of India. Indian democracy, as it developed after Independence in 1947, retained the essentials of the feudal social structure in politics as well. The big landlords in the rural sector and the moneyed class in the towns appropriated the power politics in Haryana as well as in other states of the Union of India. Some individuals did come up in leading or subsidiary positions, but they soon joined the class of ruling families by quickly becoming as rich as their rivals. It is the privileged two or three families, or a maximum of five or six, in every state which have been ruling the state by turns; others are left with no choice but to become the followers of one or the other of these bigwigs. It is these very bigwigs who would get the hold of the various political parties. If the national parties did not allow them a free hand, they would float their own outfits and contest elections on their own. Thus, from the royal to the ruling families, from the colonial to the postcolonial period, there has been no change in the social and political structures of the states.

In Haryana, the rotation has been among, largely, the three Lals and their families – Ch. Devi Lal's, Ch. Bansi Lal's, Ch. Bhajan Lal's. Others who got a chance to head the state govt., Rao Birender Singh and now Ch. Bhupinder Singh Hooda, have also joined the ruling elite, and their sons have followed to make a bid for power in the future. Others, like Ch. Samsher Singh and son, Ch. Birender Singh, but not yet the son, are very close to making it to the top. One day, they may also make it to the top. In short, the scepter travels within this close circle; it remains inaccessible to the rest of the populace.

Whatever the individual destiny at a given time, it is these half a dozen families that have become the big players of Haryana politics, and it is they who make or mar the fortunes of different political parties. The families of Ch. Devi Lal and Ch. Bhajan Lal in western Haryana, of Ch. Bansi Lal and Rao Birender Singh in southern Haryana, of Ch. Bhupinder Singh Hooda, Ch. Birender Singh and Ch. Surjewala in central Haryana, remain in the forefront of Haryana politics. Others who come to matter in the subsidiary circle are the Jindals of Hisar operating both at Hisar and Kurukshetra, the Maans of Karnal, and Rao Inderjit Singh.

There are others who have individual importance, but because of their being in the lower order of the power structure in terms of caste or community have not been able to make it to the top, room at the top being always limited. These are Captain Ajay Singh of Rewari, Kumari Selja and Sh. Lachhman Dass Arora of Sirsa, Sardar Harpal Singh and son from Tohana, Ch. Nirmal Singh of Ambala, Ch. Karan Singh Dalal of Faridabad, Sh. Ram Bilas Sharma of Mahindergarh, the Bhadanas of Faridabad, Ch. Tayab Hussan and son of Tawru, Ch. Khursid Ahmed of Mewat, etc. All these families are in the business of politics, making it a whole–time occupation, investing all their energies in strengthening their citadels in the small state of Haryana.

Returning to the period of 1991-96, this phase saw the exit of Ch. Bansi Lal from the Congress Party, as also of Ch. Birender Singh.Ch. Bhajan Lal's rise to capture absolute power in the state led to the fall of his arch rival, Ch. Bansi Lal. The latter was pushed to the wall, left with no option but to leave the party. For these big players stay loyal to their political parties only so long as they remain in privileged positions. The moment they are marginalized, they bid farewell to the party and look for either an opening in a rival party or float an outfit of their own.

There being only the Lok Dal as an alternate ruling force outside of Congress, Ch. Bansi Lal could not find shelter there. For neither he nor Ch. Devi Lal and his son, Ch. Om Parkash Chautala, would entertain the idea of being together. Like the bulls ruling their own territories in each village, these bulls of Haryana politics would not permit entry of another in their respective domains. Subordinate species are welcome, but not those of equal rank. The BJP, another political party in Haryana, which, to capture power, has to play the second fiddle to one of the non-Congress parties, could not be Ch. Bansi Lal's choice. Having the reputation of being a trader's party, the BJP would not suit Ch. Bansi Lal as he would not be owned by his own community of Jats. He had to secure the most crucial support of the peasantry, especially the Jats; only then could he hope to make a bid for the top position. So, he finally floated his own outfit called the Haryana Vikas Party.

The other member of the ruling clan, Ch. Birender Singh, was also marginalized systematically by his rival Ch. Bhajan

Lal. Defeating Ch. Birender Singh in the game of winning the majority of MLA's on his side was not enough for Ch. Bhajan Lal; it was necessary for him to finish to the extent possible the potential rival of the future. A defeated rival often is more dangerous than the one who has not tasted the fall, for the former turns a terrible revenger. Perhaps Ch. Birender Singh is not made of that sterner stuff, but Ch. Bhajan Lal is not one who would leave any scope for a possible subversion. Sh. Narsimah Rao's concerted attempt at the Centre to marginalize Smt. Sonia Gandhi and her siblings, and Ch. Bhajan Lal's intense effort to make Ch. Birender Singh a subdued Subedar left the loyalists of the Gandhi family with no choice but to quit the Congress Party.

Thus, Ch. Birender Singh joined the splinter group of the Congress Party called the Tewari Congress. This small formation included Congress leaders like Sh. Narain Dutt Tewari, Sh. Arjun Singh, Sh. Natwar Singh. In Haryana, Ch. Birender Singh and his men joined the new outfit. Among Ch. Birender Singh's friends and followers was Dr Ram Parkash who, initially a member of Ch. Bhajan Lal's Cabinet formed in 1991, was dropped after a year or so. Ironically, Dr Ram Parkash later became the Working President of Haryana Congress, and Ch. Bhajan Lal, the President, feeling marginalized, had to resign from his position, and his resignation was readily accepted. History does repeat itself as Hegel said long ago, the rise and fall of rulers being a regular phenomenon, just like the rising and setting of the sun. As T.S. Eliot, an American poet in the early twentieth century, has so beautifully said,

> History has many cunning passages, contrived corridors
> And issues, deceives with whispering ambitions,
> Guides us by vanities. Think now

She gives when our attention is distracted
And what she gives, gives with such supple confusions
That the giving famishes the craving. (Eliot, 19)

Leaving the repetitive historical happenings to a later recount, we may return to the two important exits during the early 1990's. While the exit of Ch. Birender Singh and a few of his friends and followers proved only short-lived, for he along with his men returned to the parent party when Smt. Sonia Gandhi agreed to take over the command of the Congress Party in 1996. She had assumed the driver's seat at a time when the party tickets for the Haryana Assembly election as well as for the election to the Parliament were being decided. What happened in those two elections we shall take up later. For the present, we need to dwell upon the other, and more important, exit of Ch. Bansi Lal, which event changed, though temporarily, the course of Haryana politics.

Once out of the Congress Party, Ch. Bansi Lal was faced with the possible prospect of going into oblivion. He had before him the examples of Rao Birender Singh, of Pandit Bhagwat Dayal Sharma, and of Professor Sher Singh. But he also had before him the examples of Sir Chhotu Ram and Ch. Devi Lal who emerged greater leaders outside the Congress fold. In the neighbouring state of U.P., there was the example of another Jat leader, Ch. Charan Singh. But Ch. Bansi Lal also knew that he did not have in him the qualities of these leaders, their ability to attract masses, to endear them, to make masses their followers. If anything, Ch. Bansi Lal had been until then an anti-masses leader. Like Coriolanus in Roman history, Ch. Bansi Lal would rather prefer isolated glory to mass leadership – a matter of temperament.

The memories of the Emergency Period had not wholly faded from the people's minds. Ch. Bansi Lal's autocratic style of functioning, his short temper, his touch-me-not attitude in public, all stood against him. Besides, there was the challenge of funding, urgently needed to raise a new party. Outside the established parties like the Congress or the Communist, the only way one could keep a party going, a single leader's outfit, like Ch. Charan Singh's or Ch. Devi Lal's, was to remain in constant contact with the electorate, which required continuous mobility, which in turn required finances. All this seemed an uphill task to Ch. Bansi Lal at that moment. But left with no choice, he opted for the inevitable.

As for a financer, Ch. Bansi Lal found it in Sh. Om Parkash Jindal of Hisar, an industrialist of repute in the country, who was an old contact of Ch. Bansi Lal. At this juncture, Sh. Jindal was more than willing to join Ch. Bansi Lal because of the rising challenge to his business in Hisar from Ch. Bhajan lal and his son-in-law, Sh. Anoop Bishnoi. Although new in the steel business, Ch. Bhajan lal's son-in-law was able to pose a local threat to Sh. Jindal because of the strong support he had been enjoying from the Haryana government. Ch. Bhajan Lal's long standing in power politics (since 1968) had consolidated the business interests of his son-in-law. So, Sh. Jindal happily joined Ch. Bansi Lal, going all out to financially support the new venture. A simple person with rural habits, but a business tycoon, Sh. Jindal provided the new political party of Ch. Bansi Lal, the Haryana Vikas Party, the wheels that gained momentum with time. Once the financial worry was overcome, Ch. Bansi Lal's immediate task was to collect and create a network of cadres all over the state.

This second task was averse to Ch. Bansi Lal's temperament. But his younger son, Ch. Surinder Singh, though not quite amiable, had it in him to work hard and win friends. So, he set about the job, collecting on his side all those estranged from their respective parties – the Lok Dal and the Congress. During his long span in power as Chief Minister and then as Union Minister, since 1968, Ch. Bansi Lal, more so his son, had been able to have a band of loyalists who now, when the need arose, readily walked out of the parent party and joined the new dispensation. This group included prominent personalities like Sh. Mani Ram Godara from Hisar, a long-time Bishnoi leader, rival to Ch. Bhajan Lal; Ch. Shyam Chand, a long-time Minister in Ch. Bansi Lal's Cabinet, his trusted and learned lieutenant, and a scheduled caste from Gohana; Ch. Manphool Singh, a well-known figure in Jhajjar, Ch. Om Parkash Beri from Rohtak, and several more of varying opolitical status. The company of these known faces gave Ch. Bansi Lal a certain base in several pockets of the state.

Also came to Ch. Bansi Lal's fold all those who had decided to stay on Ch. Charan Singh's side when Ch. Devi Lal formed his own Indian National Lok Dal. This group included Ch. Kanwal Singh of Hisar, from a well-known political family, his father Captain Ranjit Singh having been a Minister long-time ago; Ch. Balbir Singh Grewal of Bhiwani, who was an MLA from 1982 to 1987; Ch. Kulbir Singh Malik from Jind, who, too, was an MLA twice between 1982 and 1991; Ch. Kitab Singh Malik of Gohana, also a two-time MLA between 1982 and 1991; Shri Sahib Singh Saini of Kurukshetra, who, too, had been an MLA from 1982 to 1987; and so many more not so well known, but active workers in the field, who would be an asset to any party. This group further strengthened the new party, giving it wider prospects of acceptability among the electorate.

An equally important group of leaders that came from Ch. Devi Lal's own Lok Dal, consisted of all those ousted by the tough leadership of Ch. Devi Lal's elder son, Ch. Om Parkash Chautala, who, meanwhile, had taken over the management of the party. Although formally his father remained the President of INLD, Ch. Om Parkash Chautala called the shots without any interference even from his own father. His two brothers, Ch. Ranjit Singh, one-time Minister in Ch. Devi Lal's Cabinet, and Ch. Partap Singh, one-time MLA long before, were already out of the party, a sole family concern for all practical purposes, just as most regional parties are, be it the Socialist Party of Sh. Mulayam Singh Yadav, the Bahujan Samaj Party of Smt. Mayavati, the Shiromani Akali Dal of Sardar Parkash Singh Badal, the National Conference of Seikh Farooq Abdula, the Rashtriya Janata Dal of Sh. Laloo Prasad Yadav, or the AIDMK of Km. Jai Lalitha. These disgruntled elements of the INLD included Ch. Jai Parkash of Jind, a short-time Minister of State in Sh. Chander Shekhar's Union Cabinet in 1990; Smt. Krishna Gahlawat of Sonepat who became an MLA and a Minister in 1987; Sh. Satbir Singh Kundoo of Panipat; Ch. Karan Singh Dalal of Faridabad, and several more with strong political backgrounds.

One of these political figures, Ch. Jai Parkash of Jind, deserves a special mention here, because his desertion from the INLD had a certain significance of its own. A one-time head of the Lok Dal's notorious Green Brigade, a counterpart of the Youth Congress, Ch. Jai Parkash had risen to that status by virtue of his own personal courage. Rising from a humble background, with no family or financial advantage, he had made it to the Parliament, to the Union Cabinet, and then to a leadership of sorts, all because of his personal effort, showing exceptional courage, fearing no danger from foes or friends. His siding with Ch. Bansi Lal brought on this side a band of toughs who removed the fear of Ch. Om Parkash Chautala's men from the minds of those who wanted to oppose the politics of INLD but needed someone to give them shelter. This shelter the brave young man, Ch. Jai Parkash, provided.

Coming into the limelight during the *Naya Yudh* beginning 1985, Sh. Jai Parkash, an ordinary lad, got close to Ch. Om Parkash Chautala, secured the Lok Dal ticket to contest the election from Hisar Parliamentary Constituency in 1989, and became a Minister of State in Sh. Chander Shekhar's government.Ch. Om Parkash Chautala, being one of the key players in toppling Sh. V.P. Singh's government and installing in place the government of Sh. Chander Shekhar, could get this high position for his loyalist, Ch. Jai Parkash, although there were several senior people in the rebels' camp that came to power. Later, the disciple grew oversize and crossed over to Ch. Bansi Lal's camp to assert his new-found identity. His Green-Brigade label helped Ch. Jai Parkash, and more so Ch. Bansi Lal, who desperately needed all sorts of help to become competitive in the race for power. Armed with the money power of Shri Om Parkash Jindal and the muscle power of Ch. Jai Parkash, Ch. Bansi Lal gained confidence to challenge both the Lok Dal as well as the Congress headed respectively by Ch. Devi Lal and Ch. Bhajan Lal. Thus, the battle royal between the three Lals was round the corner.

Yet another electoral force that joined Ch. Bansi Lal's camp was the Bharatiya Kisan Union. This Union, though a staunch supporter of Ch. Devi Lal for a long time, more so since the days of *Naya Yudh,* had been annoyed by Ch. Devi Lal's elder son, Ch. Om Parkash Chautala. Although a great organizer of the party cadre and a powerful orator, he has the knack to annoy people, being rather domineering in his dealings with his supporters. At times, he would not brook even suggestions. Given to enjoying total loyalty of the party's rank and file, including even MLA's and Ministers, he had started expecting the same from whoever came to the party fold, even to extend outside support. No one could browbeat or blackmail him. Ch. Devi Lal, on the contrary, was a simple and straightforward person – the reason why he was often deceived and ditched by people, even by those whom he groomed and raised to higher positions.

One more powerful social force that extended support to Ch. Bansi Lal was the Arya Samaj, the reason being the former's slogan for imposing total prohibition from the day he was elected to power. Whether the slogan was a condition for support from the Arya Samajis or Ch. Bansi Lal's on his own thought of it as an expedient political measure cannot be stated with certainty, for both Ch. Bansi Lal's men as well as the Arya Samajis stake claim to raising the slogan and making it an election issue. Whoever thought of the timely slogan, it proved the most powerful weapon in Ch. Bansi Lal's armour to defeat his rivals. The slogan for total prohibition attracted the village women in large numbers who otherwise would vote wherever their husbands or patriarchs voted. The slogan proved a masterly stroke in the election to the Haryana Assembly in 1996.

A deciding factor in forming Ch. Bansi Lal's government was, of course, his alliance with the BJP. In the history of Haryana politics, no non-Congress government has ever been formed without an alliance with the BJP, before or after the election. When the matter of alliance was to be decided by the BJP, there were two views at the party headquarters in Delhi, as well as in the local unit in Haryana. One view was to ally with the Lok Dal of Ch. Devi Lal, the other favoured an alliance with Ch. Bansi Lal. Although Ch. Bansi Lal and Ch. Surinder

Singh had their own contacts in the BJP's central as well as state leadership, Dr Sarup Singh, a well-known friend of Ch. Bansi Lal, played a decisive role.

Ever since his days in the Rajya Sabha between 1978 and 1984, Dr Sarup Singh had developed a good equation with Shri Lal Krishan Advani, whose position in the BJP was very strong in 1996. So Ch. Bansi Lal got the blessings of Ch. Advani and Smt. Sushma Swaraj, who tilted the wavering scale of the BJP in his favour, and helped him muster a majority in the House. With 33 MLA's of his own and about a dozen of the BJP, it was not difficult for Ch. Bansi Lal to attract a few independents and form the government. So he easily succeeded in raising his tally beyond the required strength of 46 in a House of 90.

The Congress Party was thus humbled in the Haryana Assembly election of 1996, and more so Ch. Bhajan Lal, who had almost a free hand in choosing candidates for the different constituencies. Most of his followers lost in the battle of the ballot, and those who won were mostly his detractors. The total tally on the Congress side reached around the mark of ten. Ch. Bhajan Lal's woes compounded with the Congress losing in the 1996 election to Parliament as well.

The BJP, supported by several small parties, formed the government in Delhi with Sh. Atal Bihari Vajpai as its Prime Minister. The government, however, fell after a few days, followed by the formation of a Third-Front Government, supported by the socialists and communists in the main, but also by the regional parties from various states like Tamil Nadu, Andhra Pradesh, Assam, Punjab, etc. This Janata Dal-led government was headed by Sh. I.k. Gujral, a gentleman politician, in the first nine or ten months, followed by another government of the same alliance but headed by Sh. H.D. Dev

Gowda, who had earlier remained restricted to the state politics of Karnataka.

Returning to the Haryana of 1996, the two other contestants, and the major ones– the Congress and the Indian National Lok Dal – were humbled, in that both fell far short of the numbers needed to even consider making a bid to form the government. In the Congress Party, the defeat gave the detractors of Ch. Bhajan Lal, such as Ch. Birender Singh, Ch. Bhupinder Singh Hooda, and Ch. Samsher Singh Surjewala, an opportunity to work against his dominance and stake claims to the leadership of the legislature party. In such a situation of humiliating defeat, the party High Command is always inclined to sobriety and is found receptive to stories against the defeated – in politics, accusations and counter -accusations are interesting fictions rather than hard facts. The leadership question was decided in favour of Ch. Bhupinder Singh Hooda, who was for the first time elected to the State Assembly, being for a long time in the politics of Parliament, continuously winning three elections from Rohtak constituency, twice defeating the tallest Lok Dal patriarch, Ch. Devi Lal.

The Indian National Lok Dal was comparatively better placed, in that it had over 20 MLA's, whereas the Congress Party had just 9 or 10. Ch. Om Parkash Chautala became the leader of the opposition, hoping to topple the government at an appropriate time. His skills in oratory and organization were well-known, but not in maneuvering MLA's. It is, in fact, Ch. Bhajan Lal, who has had the reputation of being the master maneuverer of MLA's. But this time the tally of the Congress Party was so small in the House of 90 – just 9 – that he would not dare plan such a move. Besides, he was not heading the party in or outside the House. No one would take any trouble in politics to prepare the path to the crown for someone other than himself. Known more for snatching than sparing the crown for another, Ch. Bhajan Lal would be the last person to extend such a courtesy to any of his rivals within his own party.

It was in such a scenario that Ch. Bansi Lal became the Chief Minister of Haryana for the fourth time in 1996 – the earlier occasions being in 1968, 1972, 1986. This time, the seat was far from soft and secure, compared to his earlier elevations to this chair at the top. He could no longer hope to adopt his usual role of a domineering, even dictatorial, democratic ruler. With his far smaller number of MLA's than the required number, he had to keep in good humour his partner, the BJP, as well as the stray individuals not given to any sort of discipline. Certainly not a situation to Ch. Bansi Lal's liking! But he was in no position to have it otherwise.

11

Ch. Bansi Lal's Fourth Coming (1996-1999)

Famed for being a man of his word and reputed as a decisive and determined ruler of the state, Ch. Bansi Lal took no time to implement his promised measure of prohibition. He ordered a total ban on the use of liquor in public places, including bars and restaurants. For a while, things sounded quite sober, women more happy than men, the reason for this being their bearing the brunt of getting a beating from drunken husbands and making do with meager means of subsistence. But for a state like Haryana, in fact for any state, it ws too good to last for long. Soon, the cracks started appearing in the fortificatory walls; stories started doing the rounds about people in power, Ministers and MLA's, their friends and relatives, patronizing the smuggling of liquor.

New and newer ways got invented in no time; plastic bags and bottles appeared, as also devious ways of transporting them to villages. Soon we heard of networks of mafia created to such a perfection that home deliveries came into practice, no one needing to take the trouble of searching for safe places. The state machinery, rather than countering the mafia moves, was facilitating the free flow of the demon drink, the elixir of life, as an Urdu poet called it.

Poor Ch. Bansi Lal was helpless. The Chief Minister of the state, the man known for his dictatorial administration, now found himself reduced to a silent spectator. People found it hard to believe whatever was happening in the state, but it was happening, and if not in broad daylight, decidedly in the twilight of a setting sun. Names were being mentioned in private, often even in the press, of ministers and their men, belonging to both the BJP and the HVP, indulging in boot legging. In this depressing phase of Indian democracy, starting from the 1970's, becoming more depraved in the 1990's, most legislators came into politics with no illusions about their agendas : They were there to gain power in the business of politics, to become so strong that they remain in the political arena, pushing their personal interests further with every success in the battle of ballots.

The phenomenon of prohibition shattering on the bedrock of bourgeois democracy was nothing new; Haryana was not the first state to have tasted the fruits of failure in imposing total prohibition in the state. Gujrat had experienced it for a long time, where the joke had been that if one needed whisky, he could obtain it from the police station. Such jokes are hard to be taken as truth, but they do point to the failure of the system of governance. Even in America, when prohibition was tried in the 1920's, it failed. Prohibition had to be abolished, but the mafia it had created stayed on, which, in various forms, still continues to operate in that land of plenty.

In Haryana, too, the experiment of prohibition proved a failure, and it gave birth to the mafia, which operates today in one form or another. A large army of unemployed youth was recruited and trained in the dubious operation of smuggling, offering exposure to criminal activities from stealing to stabbing, from faking to firing. This army, though no longer organized and networked, does remain in operation even today; it is scattered in small groups, and lives by the crimes of looting and robbery, extortion and elimination.

What Ch. Bansi Lal was known for – development – was now denied to the state, for the simple reason that the main source of revenue in this state – excise – was gone. Ch. Bansi Lal thought of several alternate sources of revenue, and took recourse to the desperate measures like raising the registration fee to 15%, selling even V.I.P. (small) numbers for cars, etc., for a price. These measures did not count for much compared to the huge loss of the excise revenue. Beside, Ch. Bansi Lal earned unpopularity for taking these desperate measures. Health and education sectors became the casualties. Recruitments in universities and colleges were banned, reducing the required strength to a bare minimum, ultimately affecting the quality of teaching and research. Even schools felt the pinch with no new recruitments taking place. All these factors further eroded the base of Ch. Bansi Lal's party. His followers started looking for alternate political shelters. They were beginning to see the writing on the wall.

Not given to entertaining any request from his MLA's, Ch. Bansi Lal found himself forced to overlook the anti-people activities of his worthy colleagues. Quite a few of them indulged in malpractices, such as plying buses in the private sector, paying no taxes fixed by the state. Other practices of the type followed, with most MLA's in the ruling coalition looking for benefits and profits from whatever means their position of power could make possible. Ch. Bansi Lal, known for his aversion to such practices by his own MLA's, had to turn his eyes to the other side. A man known for development now had to remain content with the ruins of development he had once got done swiftly and sternly. Now, the same roads he got laid in the 1970's looked like their own ghosts. Electricity, once the pride of Haryana, was now available for only a few hours a day. People doubted if Ch. Bansi Lal was the same dynamic person who had earlier earned the name of the maker of modern Haryana, or was he a ghost of that man?

The people's representative, the MLA's, are the most sensitive weathercocks of the people's mood. In the third year of Ch. Bansi Lal's fourth tenure as Chief Minister, they sensed the inevitable change of fortunes approaching. Once sure their chances in the next election are bleak, these men, faceless for most of the time during the five years, can do magical exercises of making 'u' turns or bending backward, depending upon which exercise would ensure their return to the House they hate to visit unless required by the mandatory session after every six months. That mandatory sitting, too, they reduce to two or three days, often even a single day. It was not an act causing surprise to many when seventeen of Ch. Bansi Lal's MLA's walked out of his camp and pitched a new one of their own close to that of the Indian National Lok Dal headed by Ch. Om Parkash Chautala. The people of Haryana wait for such an exciting situation, for the five years of routine drift makes them sick to the bones. It is the election time that they like most.

The author recalls an incident that would amply illustrate this inordinate itch for elections in the rural folk of Haryana. Once when the author was MLA he was invited by a local philanthropist to be the Chief Guest at a function in one of the villages of Sonepat where he would dole out free gifts of TV, etc., to the village Panchayat provided the village folk agreed to make a unanimous choice and not have elections for the position of The Sarpanch. The other members of the Panchayat the Sarpanch would then nominate.

The philanthropist said he had negotiated the deal with the candidates wanting to contest the election to the position of the Sarpanch. Seeing some prospects of a new wave the philanthropist had declared that he would donate several gifts of daily use to the Panchayat whichever village adopted his plan of no-elections and chose unanimously their head-panchayati. The author saw some enthusiasm among a section of the villagers, but quite a few seemed not so enthusiastic. When the philanthropist had made his grand speech, explaining what gifts would follow the unanimous choice of the Sarpanch, an old man stood up and asked the speaker as to the cost of his gifts to the Panchayat. When the amount was mentioned, the old man said, "All right, then. You have this amount from me here and now and go back home with your charity. It is once in five years that we have this excitement, and you have come here to kill it."

So, the larger prospect of a state-wide excitement seemed around the corner now in 1999, when these 17 MLA's of Ch. Bansi Lal's ruling party went over to the opposition side to form a new government, with all these worthies getting berths in the state Cabinet of Ch. Om Parkash Chautala. Actually, these seventeen wanted to form their own Cabinet to be supported by the INLD of Shri Chautala. But hurdles came. One was that with several aspirants to the top post of Chief Minister, the deserters could not make a quick choice. Another was that Shri Chautala was not the one who would miss a chance of grabbing the coveted position. He was a tough customer when it came to making a political deal. Facing the prospect of an early election, having no chance as independents or a new party, these seventeen perforce had to agree to the leadership of Ch. Om Parkash Chautala who would be the new Chief Minister of the state. But all this followed after an interlude-- a drama of sorts, or a short dramatic episode.

Pushed to the wall Ch. Bansi Lal desperately sought shelter in the Congress camp from which he had been ousted and which he had been despising most, making uncharitable remarks even against the most sacrosanct person of the Congress Party – its president, Smt Sonia Gandhi. Any kind of remarks, however, are no consideration with the political parties when it comes to capturing power in the state or at the Centre. Instances of Ch. Charan Singh and Shri Chander Sekhar are there, and so are numerous other instances in the states of the Indian Union. So Ch. Bansi Lal's bitter remarks against the mightiest of the mighty in the Congress Party was no matter, when supporting him would ensure the party a share in the state power and a prospect of forming its own government after a while. Ch. Bhupinder Singh Hooda, the leader of the Congress Legislative Party in Haryana at the time, at once welcomed the humbled Ch. Bansi Lal, striking some sort of deal for power sharing in the state.

The deal was that for the moment the Congress would bail out Ch. Bansi Lal, and keep him as the Chief Minister of the state, but after a while – a few months, that is – either he would merge his HVP with his parent party, the Congress, or he would step down from the top position in favour of Ch, Bhupinder Singh Hooda, the leader of the Congress Party in the state Assembly. For the moment, the govt. of Ch. Bansi Lal was saved. The Congress MLA's combined with as many independents and raised the tally to the required number of 46. But the arrangement did not work for long. Something went wrong behind the scenes. Ch. Bansi Lal showed reluctance to the proposal for merging his HVP with the Congress Party. He also showed an equally strong reluctance to handing over the charge to Ch. Bhupinder Singh Hooda before the next election due in 2001. As the two parties preferred to stick to their respective stands, the arrangement broke down, with the Congress Party withdrawing its support to Ch. Bansi Lal's government. What Ch. Bansi Lal thought had been put aside for sometime to pass came quickly; he had to quit and leave the field to Shri. Chautala.

The Congress Party had hoped that the election would follow their withdrawal. But the expected did not happen. On the contrary, the band of deserters, now frightened by the prospect of a sure election, quickly agreed to have Ch. Om Parkash Chautala as Chief Minister, with some of them, not all, accommodated in the new Cabinet. The new arrangement seemed as shaky as the earlier one. There was uneasiness on both sides – the INLD as well as the band of defectors. The inevitable took place sooner than the defectors had expected. They did not quite know the capabilities Shri Chautala had in playing the murky game of politics. In fact, not even those close to him in his own party could fully comprehend these capabilities. It is always the situation that reveals a man. And here was the one that revealed the full potential of Ch. Om Parkash Chautala as a politician. He became the Chief Minister and accepted the lot of the defectors only after subdueing them, making them surrender to his will.

Ch. Om Parkash Chautala, as well as others, knew the inevitable could not be kept on hold for long: The election had to take place a year before the due date. Shri. Chautala could also sense the change in the people's mood much before the due date. He could very well see that people by and large were feeling rather disenchanted with the Congress. Initially, people were in a mood to bring back the Congress to power. The rotation demanded it. The Jat Chief Minister Ch. Bansi Lal, no longer in the Congress, must make way to the non-Jat-aspirations. It was Ch. Bhajan Lal, who had emerged in Haryana as the symbol of the non-Jat aspirations. He alone, the non-Jat communities thought, could ensure their share in the power structure of the state. He brought back the balance by favouring the non-Jats during his tenure, just as Ch. Devi Lal or his son, Ch. Om Parkash Chautala favoured the Jats during their regime. Ch. Bansi Lal was not known for caste politics when he was in the Congress. But now out of the Congress, heading his own new outfit called the HVP, he had to take recourse, per force, to the settled politics of the state –favouring the community Ch. Bhajan Lal disfavoured.

Why the people turned to Ch. Om Parkash Chautala in the election of 2000, and turned away from the Congress, is not easy to explain, for the change had come about rather quickly. The author had heard the people's voice when Ch. Bansi Lal's government fell; they clearly favoured the Congress, perhaps for rotation's sake, wanting a non-Jat leader to head the government. Whether Ch. Bhupinder Singh Hooda's leadership of the Legislature Party played the trick, or the manner in which the Congress first supported Ch. Bansi Lal and then withdrew support irked the people, is hard to say. But a change of mood did take place, and the change happened rather rapidly. People could be heard discussing or indicating that the Congress had lost the game. If Ch. Bhupinder Singh Hooda was to replace Ch. Om Parkash Chautala, who replaced Ch. Bansi Lal, the non-Jat voters, it seems, thought it would be too long a span of the Jat dominance.

In a situation where the Congress for some reason seemed to betray the non-Jat aspirations, the non-Jat communities always favoured the non-Congress combination. While the urban voters would, in such a situation, prefer the BJP to the Congress, the rural non-Jats would back up the BJP ally, the Lok Dal. That had been the pattern of politics in the state ever since its inception. The traditional alliance of the Lok Dal and the BJP had broken only in the 1996 election because there had emerged another non-Congress party in the state – Ch. Bansi Lal's HVP. And since Ch. Bansi Lal was considered not a strong Jat-minded leader, the BJP had preferred him to the Lok Dal leader, Ch. Om Parkash Chautala. It is another matter though that Ch. Bansi Lal was forced by the logic of circumstances to tilt his favour towards the Jats in that short stint in power.

If there came about a change in the non-Congress politics, there came about a change in the politics of the Congress, too. There had now emerged in the Congress Party also a Jat contender, Ch. Bhupinder Singh Hooda, for the position of the state Chief Minister. Earlier, in 1991, this challenge had come from Ch. Birender Singh, but Ch. Bhajan Lal had defeated that challenge and retained the rotatory character of the state politics – the rotation between the Jat and the non-Jat Chief Minister. Ch. Bhupinder Singh Hooda's challenge, though raised on the same plank of the majority community of Jats, was more formidable, coming as it did from the hard-core belt of the Jats. The Rohtak district, from where Ch. Bhupinder Singh Hooda hails, has traditionally been known as an area of the aggressive Jats who have habitually dominated others leaving no room for others to appropriate power, be it the unit of the village or the state. This factor might have been a deterring force that influenced the non-Jat communities to change their option and favour the non-Congress alliance in 2000.

In the alternation of the power-swing, the majority of the non-Jat voters preferred, every five years, the BJP to the Congress, and the Congress to the BJP. The reason for this urge or itch for change was, of course, neither emotional nor whimsical. No government has, in the real sense of the term, been a people's government. Each political outfit came to power on the wave of people's dissatisfaction with the former, or riding the wave of a slogan, and did little to address the real problems of the electorate. Faced with Hobson's choice, people were left with no option but to vote for a change every time, whatever change that would be. The only change they could see would always be a new set of people cornering the privileges and the positions of power. This set off power grabbers is, of course, never very large. The overwhelming majority of people have to remain content with the same poor fate, whatever be the change.

Be it as it may, in the election of 2000, Ch. Om Parkash Chautala's INLD and the BJP once again captured power in the state, but with a difference. The difference was that in that election Shri Chautala got the majority in the House and could form the government without the participation of the BJP. He did, of course, make repeated offers that the BJP could share power in the state, but the BJP stayed away. The reason was the treatment Shri Chautala had meted out to them during the election process. He had played tough, being for the first-time the undisputed leader of his father's party. The father being not in good health was only to be shown at the election rallies for an emotional appeal, which was tremendous. Ch. Om Parkash Chautala knew how to use that appeal to his advantage. He spared for the BJP a smaller number of seats than they had demanded. Besides, he gave them mostly those seats where the BJP hardly had any chance of winning. Above all, when the crux came, he put up independent candidates against the BJP's lot and succeeded in defeating quite a few of them. As a result, the final tally of the BJP remained less than the double figure.

Not only that, Ch. Om Parkash Chautala had played tricks with the BJP at the Centre as well. When elections to the Parliament were held thrice between 1996 and 2000, Shri Chautala had extended and withdrawn his support to the BJP more than once. With no clear majority to either the Congress Party or the BJP, the latter had made a bid to form the govt., and had succeded too, but only to last for a short while. In those difficult moments of frequent trials of strength, Sh. Chautala had kept the BJP guessing, and supported it only when it suited him or only after extracting a price. This had also irked the BJP's central leadership a good deal. They no longer wanted any more dealings with Ch. Om Parkash Chautala's party.

On his side, Ch. Om Parkash Chautala had not forgotten the BJP's preference for Ch. Bansi Lal in the 1996 election. It was for the first time that the BJP had broken the traditional alliance between the two. So, the bitterness on Shri. Chautala's side was no less. Known for his tough dealings and subtlety in settling scores, he could not have found a better opportunity than the election of 2000 to take revenge upon the BJP. It was the best time for him to settle old scores because he knew the majority of voters were disenchanted with Ch. Bansi Lal and were warry of the Congress because of there being a clear prospect of Ch. Bhajan Lal's replacement by the upcoming Jat leader, Ch. Bhupinder Singh Hooda, as Chief Minister, if the party was voted to power. Seeing for himself a clear edge in the election prospects, Ch. Om Parkash Chautala went all out, with an exceptional confidence, and collected a majority of seats for his party.

Ch. Om Parkash Chautala had made attempts to emerge as leader of the Lok Dal Party and capture power between 1989 and 1991 when his father, Ch. Devi Lal, had moved to Delhi to become the Deputy Prime Minister of India. But every time he made an attempt, he was checkmated by the forces within his own party, forces that included his own brothers, Ch. Ranjit Singh and Ch. Partap Singh, and close friends, like Ch. Virender Singh and Ch. Sampat Singh. Ch. Devi Lal was his own master during that period and these friends and relations had access to him to make out a case against the leadership of Ch. Om Parkash Chautala. No wonder that he had been sworn in thrice as Chief Minister during that short span and had resigned as many times, remaining in power only for days and months. Now all that was over. Ch. Devi Lal was no longer in a position to make any assertion. The brothers had been eased out of the party. As for the friends, while Ch. Virender Singh had gone over to the Congress, Ch. Sampat Singh had been subdued to survive only in servitude. Decidedly, Ch. Om Parkash Chautala was now the real supremo, with no challenge from any corner in his own party. He had the opportunity now to show whatever worth he had in him as a politician and as an administrator. And he did show his worth amply during his long tenure of full five years between 2000 and 2005.

12

Ch. Om Parkash Chautala's Full Term 2000-2005

With the entire power centred in the INLD supremeo, Ch. Om Parkash Chautala, holding the reigns of both the Govt. and the party in his hands, he followed his own discretion and did little consultations with his colleagues. Sh. Chautala formed the smallest ever Cabinet in the state of Haryana with only eight Ministers. The loss to democracy was the gain to the people, as it reduced the burden of the ministerial expenditure. In the great tradition of Haryana's power politics, Ch. Om Parkash Chautala was assisted in administration of both the government and the party by his two sons.

This great tradition was initiated by the first full-term Chief Minister of Haryana, Ch. Bansi Lal, whose son, Ch. Surinder Singh, and daughter, Smt. Saroj Siwach, lent active assistance in running the affairs of the state, after the two had come of age. Later, Ch. Bhajan Lal's sons, Shri Chander Mohan and Sh. Kuldip Singh did the same when they attained adulthood.

Ch. Devi Lal, too, was assisted by his two sons, Ch. Om Parkash Chautala and Ch. Ranjit Singh. But why blame the Haryana politicians, when in other states of the Union of India the practice has been very much the same. Actually, the model was evolved by the monarchs in medieval India.

The Chautala government started on a peaceful note, but soon rumours started floating about the Ministers and MLAs not being happy about the style of functioning of the Chief Minister and his sons. Most Ministers being new, not having much experience, did not know well enough what it means to be a Minister in Haryana, or in any other state, for that matter. Sh. Hira Nand Arya, who had remained a Minister more than once and had worked with more than one Chief Minister, had once remarked to the author in the presence of several others, that in Haryana there is only one *Mantri* (minister) the Chief Minister, the others are only *santris* (guards).

Sh. Hira Nand Arya was not quite wrong, because the power of the govt. in a small state like Haryana is concentrated in the hands of the Chief Minister. We have known Ministers humouring the personal staff of the Chief Minister, sitting in the OSD's office, putting in requests for transfers, etc., even saluting the OSD and other bosses of the CM office. We have also seen Ministers going to the Chief Minister with one of the CM's sons accompanying them to recommend their cases to the father. So, what Ch. Om Parkash Chautala was doing was not new in Haryana; only some of the Ministers were not conversant with the system.

Within a few months of the formation of the Chautala govt. a revolt of sorts cropped up. A Minister, a green horn in politics, is said to have gone one evening to the I.G. (C.I.D.), considering him a brother, both being from the same caste, and disclosed that the next day the Govt. of Haryana would be their own. The Police Officer did not quite get the message and remarked that the govt. was theirs even then, as the two held key positions in the govt. The Minister then clarified that he himself would become the Chief Minister as several MLA's had decided to stage a coup, having an assurance of support from the opposition, mainly the Congress. The first-timer Minister was rather naïve, knowing not the ways of politics and police in the state. The moment the Minister left, the I.G. (C.I.D.) informed the Chief Minister about what was cooking within his own camp.

Known for his swiftness and subtlety in administration as well as organization, Ch. Om Parkash Chautala, Haryana's Chief Minister, got the band of conspirators individually tackled by police as well as partymen. While the police maintained a watch on the ambitious Ministers and MLA's, the partymen roughed up whoever could be found in private or secluded places. The would-be Chief Minister, the story goes, was roughed up in the lift while on his way to his office on the eighth floor of the Civil Secretariat in Chandigarh. Some of them are said to have been physically assaulted by the INLD enthusiasts. When asked, those allegedly roughed up gracefully denied the rumours and praised the Chief Minister and his sons as the best of their friends and benefactors. The honourable Ministers cannot, of course, be counted as liars; if they dismiss the rumours, as 'honourable men' they must be believed for what they claim or disclaim.

After this half-baked revolt was successfully curbed, all became quiet on the govt. front, and Ch. Om Parkash Chautala lived in peace with no sign of any trouble from within his own party and the government. This was no small achievement in the state of Haryana. Even a person like Ch. Bansi Lal, having the reputation of being a strong man, a stern administrator, had failed to keep his flock of Ministers and MLA's together when he was the Chief Minister between 1996 and 1999. Half of his flock had deserted him and joined hands with Ch. Om Parkash Chautala in 1999. It was also Sh. Chautala, and not Ch. Bansi Lal, who taught these seventeen men of straw the lesson they deserved. He used them when he needed them, and discarded them when he didn't. They were first lured to cosy positions, then denied tickets for the inevitable election. Ch. Om Parkash Chautala will be remembered for the lesson he taught the band of defectors. The story of 'Aya Ram, Gaya Ram', which started in 1967, defaming the new state for its murky politics, came to an end with the master stroke Ch. Om Parkash Chautala dealt to the defectors.

Another reason for the end of the phenomenon of 'Aya Ram, Gaya Ram' was, of course, the amendment to the Anti-Defection Act. The original Act introduced at the time when Sh. Rajiv Gandhi was the Prime Minister of India between 1984 and 1989, permitted defection to a group forming one third of the total legislative strength of a party. The amendment that came out later at the end of the twentieth century made the defection an impossibility, raising the required number of the defecting group to two-third of the legislative strength of a party. All the same, what Ch. Om Parkash Chautala did was a rare event in the history of Haryana politics. There is perhaps no other example of the type in any other state of the Indian Union. People found something to admire in Sh. Chautala who, after the Meham byelection in 1989, had formed an adverse opinion of his personality, considering him not laudable like his father.

But the measure he took in tackling the menace of defection was laudable, indeed.

Another praise that Ch. Om Parkash Chautala earned during his Chief Ministership between 1999 and 2005 was for the development work he did in the rural sector. Knowing full well that his stronghold was rural Haryana, he devoted his time and opened his purse (the state budget) largely for the villages. He strengthened the network of roads in the rural areas, gave the rural boys jobs in police, transport, and other avenues of employment, showing an outright preference for the ruralites, especially those from the constituencies that elected him and his sons to the Parliament and the State Assembly. Such measures cut both ways, though: If it pleased those who got benefits, it displeased those who were denied the opportunity. Shri Chautala Govt's alleged preference for the farming communities alienating the non-farming ones. Both ways, the number of those displeased and alienated became much more than the number of the beneficiaries. But that is how most regional parties operate: they consolidate their caste or community base and nourish it for further expansion whenever they capture power. So long as their own constituency remains intact, they are not bothered about the feelings and concerns of others.

Another negative aspect of the strong regime of Ch. Om Parkash Chautala was the political vendata against those who had challenged him one time or another. Among those who had to bear the brunt of his vendata included Ch. Anand Singh Dangi of Meham, Ch. Jai Parkash of Jind, Ch. Ghasi Ram Nain of the Kisan Union, etc. All the three at one time were close associates of Sh. Chautala, but they had parted company later and had actively opposed the strong man in the recent past. A still greater sufferer was Sh. Tajinder Singh Maan of Karnal who has always been the target of Ch. Devi Lal's family right from the 1970's. Every time the family came to power, this man had to face serious criminal charges, and had to pass months behind the bars. The others, too, had to spend days and months in jail. The rumours doing the round in the state at the time were that these rivals of Sh. Chautala were ill-treated by the jail authorities. Rumours are hard to verify, nor does anyone have involvement to the extent of making an investigation in such matters. Most of us remain content believing whatever the rumour mills market for public consumption. So the world goes, the world of mortal humans. But it is such rumours that go into creating public opinion even if they are baseless.

The tragedy of the tough regime of Ch. Om Parkash Chautala was that the rumour mills substituted legitimate means of information. Common people developed a deep sense of fear and tried to remained out of sight of the feared authorities, ensuring that they remain out of their minds as well. In this environment, the process of alienation of the ruling powers gets more and more accelerated, isolating them from the masses at large, barring, of course, the beneficiaries. This class of hangers-on is, however, not a large one. The constituency of the caste men, too, starts dwindling under the pressure of the winds blowing around it. After all, castes are not communities living in segregated spaces; all castes live in a mixed community, sharing the common experience of natural as well as manmade calamities.

Thus, after half the term of the Chautala government was over, people started talking about the necessity for change. The most feared person of the regime was the Chief Minister's younger son, Ch. Abhay Chautala. The elder one, Ch. Ajay

Chautala, considered comparatively soft spoken, earned a measure of popularity. Ch. Abhay Chautala may or may not have been what he had come to figure in the public perception, but it is the public opinion that finally counts in a people's democracy, where elections are held every five years, often even before. All these factors contributed to the growing unpopularity of the Chautala government, making the people strongly desirous of change.

But who should replace the strong man? Contenders in the Congress camp were several, including Ch. Bhajan lal, Ch. Bhupinder Singh Hooda, Ch. Birender Singh, Ch. Samsher Singh Surjewala as well as Surjewala the younger. On the eve of the 2005 election, the Congress Party made a change, appointing Ch. Bhajan Lal as President of the state unit, who after Ch. Bhupinder Singh Hooda's election to Parliament in 2004 had been working as leader of the legislative party. This aroused high hopes among the non-Jat communities who were deeply desirous of change.

In a small state like Haryana, a slight preference to any one caste or community in appointments, in fact, even in postings and transfers, affects the electoral fortunes of the party in power, telling at once upon the popularity of the government among those not favoured or preferred. With three years of Ch. Bansi Lal's government, followed by the six years of Ch. Om Parkash Chautala's govt., the feeling among the non-Jats was that it was their turn now to have a Chief Minister of their own. Their preference for Ch. Bhajan Lal hinged on this sentiment.

It is hard to believe, but one Superintendent of Police told a journalist in confidence that during the regime of Ch. Om Parkash Chautala there were instructions (must be oral) to the district police chiefs that no FIR would be registered against members of the Jat community, if the other party involved was from a non-Jat community. When the police officer's attention was drawn to the cases, even murder cases, registered against important people of the Jat community, such as Ch. Tajinder Singh Maan of Karnal, Ch. Anand Singh Dangi of Rohtak, and Ch. Ghasi Ram Nain of Kaithal, the officer's reply was that the matter involving these three was political, not general. Whatever be the case, the people's perception at large was that the nine years of the two Jat Chief Ministers had been partial to one community. We know that such perceptions of the public, when taken over by the rumour mills, always get magnified beyond proportions. At the same time, it is these very perceptions, right or wrong, moderate or magnified, which create a climate of opinion for or against a political party, and decide the fortunes of political leaders.

Returning to the situation in the Congress camp, on the eve of the Haryana Assembly election of 2005 majority of the people wanting a change of guard at the Haryana secretariat had their hearts fixed on Ch. Bhajan Lal. Over the years, in the small world of the state politics of Haryana, determined by caste combinations more than by party affiliations, Ch. Bhajan Lal had emerged as the lone symbol of the anti-Jat sentiments, largely supported by the Brahmins and the Punjabis, but also adopted by the smaller castes and communities traditionally given to feeling unsafe and threatened by the dominant community of Jats. The Jats, incidentally, have a tendency to look larger than their size, seemingly occupying much more space than they actually do. For instance, if a Jat gets a job or a position in the government, he would go about with a bold face telling his friends and foes how the man in power favoured him – the difference "our own man" makes. Also, if a Jat has scored a point over his rival, he would not only feel pleased, he must make the other party feel miserable. Two typical anecdotes come to mind.

Once in a village near Gohana, during the days of Ch. Chhotu Ram, a money-lender in the village had got the Jat Zaildar of that village removed through his influence with the district officer of the British Colonial government. The Zaildar reached Lahore to seek support from his leader, Ch. Chhotu Ram, who was a Minister in the Unionist Party government in Punjab, and narrated the tale how the Jat community had been insulted in his removal from Zaildarship. The leader got him reinstated. On receiving the order of reinstatement, the Zaildar went to the house of the money-lender and knocked at the door with his *lathi* (a long bamboo stick). When the owner came out, the Jat Zaildar told him, *"Tera Phoopha phir agia"* (your father's sister's husband has again come back). The money-lender, known for cleverness, only remarked, "Choudhary, don't think it was your good luck alone that brought you back to your position, a portion of our bad luck, too, remained to be suffered.

Another illustrative anecdote is that once someone needed a horse to visit a neighbouring village – those days there was no other means of prestigious transport, the only other means of transport being a bullock cart. The Jat owner of the horse expressed inability to oblige the man, because his horse was already away to another village where the owner's son had some social duty to perform. When the man had gone some distance after the negative reply, the Jat owner of the horse called the man back. The man felt pleased, thinking perhaps the horse had returned or could be available in a while. But when he reached where the owner was standing, the message he received was, "I would not have given the horse to you, even if it had not been away." The reason why the owner would not have lent his horse to the man was that the man in question had not attended his son's betrothal ceremony long ago.

Well, that is in the grain, that goes with the identity of the typical rustic Jats: the reason why they look larger than their size, spread as if all over the state. The fact of the matter is that their dominance at best is restricted to less than half the number of districts in the state. But their loud mouth, their enlarged self-esteem, their rusticity, all combine to make their presence stronger than their statistical numbers would show. Besides, their being a landed-community, their being in greater numbers in the army and the state police, makes them much more confident than any other community in Haryana. Even the higher-castes are not considered high enough by the Jats of Haryana, because in practical life they have been better off owing to their lands, feeling more safe and secure with the political privilege and power they have enjoyed right from the days of Ch. Chhotu Ram.

As the law of nature goes, action and reaction are equal and opposite. If the Jats assume a threatening posture while in power, the others silently stick together to hit back when the opportunity arrives. And the opportunity did arrive early in the year 2005. The elections were fixed in the month of February. In the distribution of the Congress Party tickets, no single leader, including Ch. Bhajan Lal, was allowed overriding preference; district-wise, the local leaders were given great weightage. As a result, besides Ch. Bhajan lal, Ch. Bhupinder Singh Hooda, Ch. Birender Singh, Ch. Surjewala, Kumari Selja, Rao Inderjit Singh, etc., all got their individual shares. Besides, all the nine (out of a total of ten) M.P'.s of the Congress were allowed to nominate one candidate each. The election, as expected, went the Congress way, and overwhelmingly so, with the Party winning 65 out of 90 seats.

An important factor in the defeat of Ch. Om Parkash Chautala's Lok Dal was also the BJP's refusal to have any alliance with the INLD. Both the parties paid the price for not striking an alliance. In the history of Haryana, as well as Punjab, no Non-Congress government has ever been formed without an alliance with the BJP. This party, considered a party of the Punjabi Hindus, both in Haryana and Punjab, though never in a position to win a large number of seats to form a government of its own, does carry a considerable influence in the urban pockets of both Punjab and Haryana. Sh. Chautala tried hard to have an alliance with the BJP. He even utilized the services of his family friend, Sardar Parkash Singh Badal heading the Shiromani Akali Dal in Punjab, and a partner of the BJP - led National Democratic Alliance at the Centre. The central leadership of the BJP, too, felt inclined to take yet another chance, to make another bid for power, by combining with the INLD. But the local leadership of the BJP, as also its rank and file, had too many bitter memories to forget them so quickly. They were ready to revolt in case the central leadership imposed an alliance with INLD. Finally, the two parties had to go it alone. The result, as expected, was that while the INLD had to be content with only 9 MLA's, all of whom, except Ch. Om Parkash Chautala, were returned from the constituencies reserved for SC/ST's , the BJP could secure only about half a dozen seats in a House of 90.

The Congress Party had a task cut out before it with the majority of MLA's favouring Ch. Bhajans Lal, but the Party wanted to bring new blood at the top. Ch. Bhajan Lal had been

Chief Minister for over 12 years earlier in three spans, but who would not like to be the Chief Minister one more time? He very much wanted the coveted seat of power and had used all his skills to muster the majority of MLAs. A meeting of the newly elected MLA's was called at Chandigarh. The nine MPs were also present. The central observers were called one by one to ascertain their views. While all the MPs except his own son voted against Ch. Bhajan Lal, he claimed that over 40 of 65 MLA's favoured him for leadership. Since the voting, in fact, was oral, only the central observes knew the real position. One thing was, of course, certain, that there was no unanimity among those consulted by the central observers. The Delhi meeting a few days later was called in the afternoon, but in the morning the MADAM had summoned Ch. Bhajan Lal at 10 Janpath and conveyed her decision to make Ch. Bhupinder Singh Hooda the Chief Minister of Haryana. The meeting was not attended by all the MLA's – about twenty are said to have stayed at Ch. Bhajan Lal's Delhi residence.

There were some among the absentees who later said that they had been forcibly detained by Ch. Bhajan Lal at his residence in Delhi. It is quite possible in politics. Equally possible is it that those claiming detention stayed willingly but changed their position with the change of fortunes. The event of Bhupinder Singh Hooda's election as leader had an interesting aspect to it. He had to work quite hard for a long time to get the position of the Chief Minister, which his father was offered even without asking for it. His father's seniority and dedication to the Congress Party had earned him that offer, which he had humbly declined, not being very ambitious. His son, though equally dedicated to the Party which he had nourished for years, was not without ambition. He wanted to become the Chief Minister and had worked hard for years to obtain it. This time he had used all the means at his command to attain his ambition. He understood the situation, saw a clear chance, and made it a point not to miss it. Such an opportunity had appeared in the life of Ch. Birender Singh in 1991. In fact, the situation then was even more favourable for him than it was this time for Ch. Bhupinder Singh Hooda. But Ch. Birender Singh lost the opportunity and lost the chance of being considered again. Maybe, he does get a chance some day, but the prospects do not look very bright. A failure in a favourable situation is much more ruinous than an ordinary failure in adverse circumstances.

So Ch. Bhupinder Singh Hooda proved his metal and got the fruit of his long struggle to bring back to Rohtak the power and glory it once enjoyed long Ago in the time of Ch. Chhotu Ram. The dominance of the old Hisar district, of which Bhiwani and Sirsa used to be Tehsils, thus came to an end. Beginning with Ch. Bansi Lal's taking over as the Chief Minister of Haryana in 1968 and ending with Ch. Om Parkash Chautala's term in 2005, the dominance of the Hisar region had remained unchallenged for almost forty years.

The regional dominance in a small state like Haryana means more jobs to the people of that region and rapid development of the towns falling in that area. It is well known that during this long span, while the towns of Bhiwni, Hisar and Sirsa developed rapidly, growing into big cities, the towns of Rohtak, Sonepat, and Jind remained neglected, witnessing not much change as urban centres. In the matter of giving jobs, the district of Rohtak and Sonepat were alleged to have been especially marked for disfavour. The successive Chief Ministers advanced the plea in private that the people of Rohtak region were already in dominance in the services, having had the advantage of being in proximity to Delhi, which made education easily accessible to them much earlier than to others. There is some truth in both these pleas. But neither pleas nor facts are as influential as public perceptions.

If we look back we can see that the game of power politics in Haryana has largely been between the districts of Rohtak and Hisar. This old rivalry between Rohtak and Hisar formed an undercurrent in the selection of the new Chief Minister of Haryana in 2005. And so did the other undercurrent of the Jat-Non-Jat antagonism in the power politics of Haryana. As in Punjab, the Congress Party had apparently decided to favour the dominant Jat community way back in 1956 when S. Partap Singh Kairon was made the Chief Minister of Punjab, sending Shri Bhim Sen Sachar as the Ambessador to Russia, so it felt compelled to adopt the same policy in Haryana. The political advantage that Ch. Chhotu Ram had secured for the Jat community in Haryana grew stronger with time. The Jat dominance in power politics continues to grow both in Haryana as well as Punjab.

Determined not to alienate this community, the Congress Party had clinched the issue of leadership after the Assembly election of 2005 in favour of Ch. Bhupinder Singh Hooda. The Jats of Rohtak region had seen that ray of hope in this election and had voted for the Congress party with much greater enthusiasm than they had done ever before. Ch. Bhupinder Singh Hooda had also pleaded with the High Command of the Congress Party that he could strengthen the party's base in the Jat belt of the state; the party's High Command was readily convinced of his plea. With all these factors in the background Ch. Bhupinder Singh Hooda took over the reigns of power in the state in March 2005. What has happened thereafter, we shall narrate in the next chapter.

13

Ch. Bhupinder Singh Hooda's Maiden Term 2005-2010

With Ch. Bhajan Lal and his truncated legislative support remaining irreconciled, the beginning of Ch. Bhupoinder Singh Hooda's regime was not quite smooth. But with his determination to make a place for himself, to consolidate his position among the MLAs and MPs as well as among the people, Ch. Bhupinder Singh Hooda took up his agenda in all seriousness and concentrated on its implementation. His focus was to commercially develop the region around Delhi, which included the areas of Gurgoan, Jhajjar, Sonepat and Faridabad districts. Soon after taking over as the Chief Minister he announced the establishment of the Rajiv Gandhi City of 'world-class education' to the north of Delhi. He also announced the creation of four Special Economic Zones around the national capital.

Although this agenda announced by the new Chief Minsiter was in keeping with the national policy of globalizing and liberalizing the ecnonomy, making it possible for the big players in business to make huge investments in Haryana, it was not to be implemented without impediments. Certain social activists and political opportunists made attempts to fish in troubled waters. But the resistance could not pick up momentum owing to the lukewarm response of the farmers who seemed happy with the price they had been offered for their land acquired by the state government. The SEZ projects are going on without much noise against it. The lone voice now remains that of Shri Kuldip Bishnoi, the younger son of Ch. Bhajan Lal, an M.P., who is already suspended from the Congress Party. Not that Shri Bishnoi, or, for that matter, his father, had ever been a friend of farmers, but his political situation demands that he must oppose whatever Ch. Bhupinder Singh Hooda's govt. does in the state.

It is interesting that compared to Haryana, West Bengal has to face such a stiff resistance from the farmers backed by the aggressive activists of the Trinamul Congress headed by Kumari Mamta Bannerji that more than once the police had to resort to firing, causing several deaths. After several months of concerted struggle, the resisting party has succeeded in compelling the West Bengal government to review its policy and come out with the statement that no land would be acquired without the prior consent of the owning farmers. The comparison calls for a close study, but our present concern being altogether different, limited to Haryana's politics, we leave it for someone else to pursue. There are other states, too, where SEZ's are being created with varying degrees of resistance experienced by the respective governments, compelling the Union Government to give a fresh look to the entire issue.

Police excesses, such as the one in handling the Honda workers strike at Gurgoan or the one seen in handling the Liberty workers' agitation at Karnal, both in 2005, did not augur well for the new regime. The new Chief Minister also had to face in the initial stages the autonomous functioning of some of his own colleagues who chose to ignore even his legitimate privileges as Chief Minister. But gradually he has gained experience and tightened his grip over things, especially administration. But there is still a feeling that the elite bureaucracy drives him its own ways. The specialists in education and agriculture, industry and technology, do remain unhappy owing to bureaucratic dominance. Made aware of this aspect of his administration, the new Chief Minister has started taking strict action against the erring officers of the elite cadres.

Returning to politics, while the other contenders for the top position of the state Chief Minsiter are either reconciled or relegated, only Ch. Bhajan Lal remains a thorn in the flesh of the Congress Party, continuing the pinpricking, threatening to launch a new political party, hoping to jeopardize the Party's chances in the next election. Now, when he and his lieutenant legislators have been expelled, having floated his new political outfit called Haryana Janhit Congress, the fight between Ch. Bhupinder Singh Hooda and Ch. Bhajan Lal has come out in the open. The latter is in the same position now in which Ch. Banshi Lal was in 1995 - struggling to survive. And the former is in the same position in which Ch. Bhajan Lal was at that time - calling the shots in the Congress Party.

Although Ch. Bhupinder Singh Hooda's Government has completed two and a half years, Ch. Om Parkash Chautala's party has got into top gear to prepare for the battle to come. One reason for the INDL's taking to activism is Sardar Parkash Singh Badal's return to power in Punjab. The reasons for Shri Chautala's optimism to make a come back in the next election are more than one. The principal reason is their belief that if

Sardar Badal can be returned to power in Punjab despite there being huge charges of corruption against him, which had led to his defeat in the last election, he is bound to stage a come back in Haryana in the next election. He only needs to wake up and be there.

The kind of political party Ch. Bhajan Lal and his son have formed is, in fact, a misnomer; for in terms of the accepted concept of the political party, the new outfit would not qualify for the nomenclature. But in the context of present-day Indian politics, most regional parties, and even some of the national parties, are only private limited companies, created and controlled by a family. We have operating at present, in several srtates of the Indian Union, so many of these political companies duly accepted by the Election Commission. From Kashmir to Kanyakumari, there is hardly a state where at least one such regional outfit is not in existence. With the National Conference in Kashmir, Shiromani Akali Dal in Punjab, Indian National Lok Dal in Haryana, Samajvadi Party, Rashtriya Lok Dal, and Bahujan Samaj Party in U.P., Rastriya Janata Dal in Bihar, Trinamul Congress in West Bengal, DMK and AIDMK in Tamil Nadu, Janata Dal (Secular) in Karnataka, etc., etc.

So, If Ch. Bhajan Lal and his son float a political outfit of their own, they will not be violating any rule of the political game being played in our country under the official umpiring of the Election Commission of India. As the saying goes, do in Rome as the Romans do. Ch. Bhajan Lal is more Indian than other Indians. In fact, he is one of the pioneers of the present-day political culture of our country. It will, therefore, only be befitting that he should be leading a form of political party entirely of free India's creation. The Congress party, too, is in the process of preparing itself for the scenario likely to emerge at the next election.

Besides this new party just floated by Ch. Bhajan Lal and his son, with the son as its leading light, there are other new challenges like the BSP to face in the next election. The son has, of course, been declaring for some time that he would be the next Chief Minister of Haryana. Whether his announcement is prophetic, only time will tell. But it is certain that this new party will pose a serious challenge to the ruling Congress party in Haryana headed by Ch. Bhupinder Singh Hooda. Those conversant with the politics of Haryana know that Ch. Bhajan Lal's Party would rely upon two factors to make a bid for capturing power in the state. One of these factors will be its slogan that both Ch. Bhupinder Singh Hooda's party as well as that of Ch. Om Parkash Chautala's would serve the interests of the dominant Jat community, and that his own new party has been formed precisely for protecting the interests of the non-Jat communities.

That there have been in succession three Jat Chief Ministers of Haryana between 1996 and 2010 – Ch. Bansi Lal (1996-1999), Ch. Om Parkash Chautala (2000-2005), and Ch. Bhupinder Singh Hooda (2005-2010) would certainly be a factor for Ch. Bhajan Lal to win favour from the non-Jat communities. While Ch. Om Parkash Chautala would not controvert it, because it would help consolidate the Jat vote for his party, Ch. Bhupinder Singh Hooda would seriouisly contest this contention with the plea that the Congress Party never played caste politics, and that the Party's secular credentials were beyond doubt. However, in the caste-ridden politics of Haryana, as well as of the country as a whole, such pleas may not be of much avail.

What can be used even in the caste-ridden politics of our country is the welfare work done for the people. There are before us two solid examples of the Congress Chief Ministers who remained in office for ten years, winning two elections in a row.

Shri Digvijay Singh of Madhya Pradesh and Smt. Shiela Dixit of Delhi would serve as sources of inspiration for Ch. Bhupinder Singh Hooda in Haryana. He seems to be fully aware of this fact, the reason why he is concentrating on developmental activities, leaving the caste politics to the older hands of Haryana politics. What worked for Shri Digvijay Singh and Smt. Sheila Dixit may work for Ch. Bhupinder Singh Hooda as well. There lies the hope that keeps him confident of himself despite serious challenges brewing in the state.

Ch. Bhupinder Singh Hooda knows that he got the leadership because he belongs to the dominant caste, and it is important for him not only to maintain the support he got in the last election but to increase it, cutting into Ch. Om Parkash Chautala's support base in the community. Until 2005 the Jats were considered the support base largely of Ch. Devi Lal and his son. But a big dent was made in that support base by Ch. Bhupinder Singh Hooda in the election of 2005 which had tilted the scale in his favour and against Ch. Bhajan Lal. In order therefore to keep intact this solid support he has to show commitment to the interests of the peasantry even stronger than was shown by Ch. Om Parkash Chautala. The first–timer Chief Minister, who made history in 2005 by breaking the hold on Haryana's power politics of the trio of three Lals – Devi Lal, Bansi Lal, Bhajan Lal – has certainly done for the farmers a few things that have been called historical by impartial observers.

The most significant step Ch. Bhupinder Singh Hooda took was to give high prices to the farmers whose farm lands are acquired by the Haryana Urban Development Authority for whatever use – for Special Economic Zones or otherwise. Earlier, the price given to the farmers used to be one-time payment, that too not even one tenth of what the present governement has paid. More important, the farmers will be paid royalty on their acquired land at the rate of fifteen thousand rupees per acre for as long as thirty three years. Such a step, it must be mentioned, had not been taken even by Ch. Chhotu Ram, considered the most ardently committed to the casue of farmers. It had not occurred even to Ch. Devi Lal, another Kisan leader still remembered for his staunch commitment to the welfare of farmers. How far this historical step will help Ch. Bhupinder Singh Hooda in beating the rival Kisan or Jat leader, Ch. Om Parkash Chautala, in the next election due in 2010, only time will tell.

Even more than the INLD of Ch. Om Parkash Chautala, the threat to the Congress Party in the next election seems to come from the new outfit of Ch. Bhajan Lal and his son, Shri Kuldip Bishnoi. By itself, this youngest party led by the youngest leader may not be of great consequence in the electoral battle for power. But combined with the BJP or the BSP, it can pose a formidable challenge to the Congress led by Ch. Bhupinder Singh Hooda. While a tie–up of the new party with the BSP seems a remote possibility, its alliance with the BJP seems plausible, although the state unity of the BJP keeps asserting to the contrary. As we know, Kumari Mayavati is seldom in favour of alliances before the election. Her contention is that the alliance partner – whichever be the party – always takes advantage of her vote bank, and is never able to transfer its own vote to the BSP. Also, since her experiment of the new social engineering (making the Brahmins her partymen and voters) has been a great success in U.P, she is keen to give it a trial in other states as well. In fact, this success has made her so ambitious that in the next election to Parliament due in 2009, she will make a serious bid to form her own government at the Centre, hoping to realize her dream of becoming the Prime Minister of India.

It also suits the new party of Ch. Bhajan Lal and his son that the BSP should contest the Haryana Assembly election independently. For whatever percentage of voters the BSP polls, the loss will be entirely of the Congress Party. And if the U.P. experiment of making the Brahmins her internal allies, sharing the same symbol and flag, power and privilege, work in other states as well, then the loss to the Congres Party will be all the more serious. Traditionally, both the Dalits and the Brahmins have been voting for the Congress. In fact, these two vote-banks have been the stable and strong base of the national party of the Congress. But if those two sections desert the giant party, the Congress, it will be reduced to a poor player. It is difficult to predict the election results at this stage, but there seems to be a tough time ahead for the Congress Party in Haryana.

The alliance between the Bhajan Lal outfit and the BJP seems rather natural for more reasons than one. The greatest common factor between the two is their common vote bank of the Punjabi Hindus. Ch. Bhajan Lal, right from his first term as Chief Minister, has been most favourably inclined towards the Punjabi Hindus, calling them his own, as his origin by birth was in Bhawalpur, now a part of Pakistan. Besides this strong tie, he has always patronised them while in power. When he toppled the govt. of Ch. Devi Lal in 1979, he had succeeded precisely because of his close affinity with the Jan Sangh faction of the Janata Party. Aslo, whenever he needed the support of some MLA's from outside his own party, some legislators of the BJP always came to his rescue. This natural affinity between the two and their long understanding in practical politics would automatically effect a union between them before the next election in Haryana due in 2010. And once that natural partnership takes place, the event will ignite a tremendous spark of enthusiasm among their voters.

The INLD of Ch. Om Parkash Chautala will have the disadvantage of there being not much room for the non-Jat leadership in his party. The prospect of there being another Jat Chief Minister after 2010 sends a shudder in the spines of the non-Jat communities in Haryana. The long span of the Jat Chief Minsiters from 1996 to 2010 has huddled together all the non-Jat communities into a solid block of voters going against all those parties that seem to hand over the reigns of power to a Jat leader. In the Congress Party, there is always room for making adjustments whenever the situation calls for a change. We know how in 1986, Ch. Bhajan Lal was suddenly asked to make way for Ch. Bansi Lal. Earlier, when Ch. Bansi Lal moved to the Centre in 1975, the leadership of the Congress government in Haryana was handed over to Lala Banarsi Das.

Of course, the same Lala Banarsi Das was made the Lok Dal Chief Minister as well when Ch. Devi Lal moved to the Centre in 1989. Both times, however, the late Lala Banarsi Das was only a proxy Chief Minsiter. The general impression among the public in Haryana, including the Jats, is that INLD is the party of the Jats. If this impression keeps away large numbers of the non-Jats voters from INLD, the same impression also makes the Jats all the more aggressive in their election compaign for the party of Ch. Om Parkash Chautala. Unlike the Congress Party's secularism, the reputed casteism of the INLD or the alleged communalism of the BJP helps the latter parties in having at least one sure and solid vote bank. Thanks to the secularism of the Congress Party that in U.P. it has been reduced to insignificance, all its earlier vote-banks snatched by the caste and community based parties. What happens in Haryana in 2010, only time will tell. But the prospects as of today, despite the good work the present government is doing, don't seem to ensure a clear victory for the Congress Party. Of course, much will depend on the kind of alliances that take place on the eve of the election of 2010. If no alliances take place, the Congress would be the sure gainer. Of late, the BJP has started showing some inclination towards INLD. The Byelection to the three Assembly constituencies of Adampur, Gohana, and Indiri will help clarify the present confusion. It will show each party's strength and indicate the possible alliances for 2010.

It will be perhaps the first Haryana election in 2010 when the contest may be between more than two serious contenders for power. Earlier, the contest has always been between the Congress Party on the one hand and a combination of two or more non-Congress parties on the other. Sensing the possible threat to the impenetrable present position, the Congress Party has adopted the Mayavati model of social engineering by appointing Ch. Phool Chand Mullana, a Dalit, as President of the Haryana Congress and making Pandit Kuldip Sharma as the Working President of the Party. By so doing, the Congress High Command seems to believe that the threat from the Mayavati party of BSP has been forestalled. How do the people view this move, only the election results would reveal.

Whoever be the President of a political party, any party, has never been taken note of by the electorate in Hayrnaa. The voters in Haryana know, as well as we do, that the Presidents are generally figure-heads. Besides, it is not the President who has to run the government of the state. By making a Punjabi the President of the INLD, Ch. Om Parkash Chautala cannot take it for granted that he has ensured the Punjabi votes for his Party, nor are the people naïve to think that the nominated President would have much to do with the running of the government if INLD won the majority of seats in the next election. The Dalit Presidnt of the Congress Party, though competent and sensible, also cannot be expected to convince the Dalit voters that he would be the Chief Minister of Haryana, if the Congress Party came to power in 2010.

The Congress Party's problem is that if a Dalit is projected as the next Chief Minsiter of the state, then the chances are that the Jats and several other farming communities would in no time extend support to the INLD of Ch. Om Parkash Chautala. What the Party has gained in ample measure, snatching a large chunk of Shri Chautala's Jat voters, by making Ch. Bhupinder Singh Hooda the Chief Minister of Haryana, would in no time evaporate into an empty vessel. No doubt, a genuine declaration of the Dalit leadership would consolidate the Congress Party's position among the Scheduled Castes, but it will also lose the stronger support of the dominant community. It is a difficult situation, indeed, with gains and losses inseparably attached to each option.

We know how such an experiment had not worked in the state of Maharashtra. The Congress Party had made Shri Sushil Kumar Sindhe the Chief Minister of Maharashtra. It was a good choice, Sindhe being an able administrator and a seasoned politician. But it annoyed the dominant community of the Marathas. It was only to please the powerful Marathas that the Congress Party had to send Sh. Sindhe to the Centre and make Shri Vishal Rao Desmukh the Chief Minister of Maharashtra. The Congress Party had tried a similar experiment in the 1970's in Punjab by making Giani Zail Singh, an OBC, the Chief

Minister of the state. Thereafter, the Congress Party has always opted for a Jat Sikh Chief Minister, be it Smt. Rajinder Kaur Bhattal or Captain Amrinder Singh, or Sardar Beant Singh. Obviously, majority and dominant caste is hard to ignore in a democracy.

In view of the above, one can see that the situation in Haryana's election of 2010 will be more complicated than it has ever been before. The only hope for the Congress Party can be an aggressive campaigning by the joint leadership of the Chief Minister and the President, showing a solidarity of not only their individual persons but also of the two social groups generally suspicious of each other. A new leadership that can attack the family-rule tradition that has gone on for decades, that can expose the monopoly of the private limited companies in poltics, that can even expose the exploiters of caste and communal sentiments, will be able to liberate the people of Haryana from the stranglehold of the feudal and communal forces backed by money and muscle power. Let us see who comes up to make a mark in the next championship for power due in 2010!

14

Parties Seasoned and Seasonal

While the game of power politics in Haryana has remained a privilege of the Congress Party on the one hand and the Lok Dal and the BJP on the other, there are always a number of other parties to be counted under the category "they also ran". In this category, too, there are some parties that are seasoned, others are only seasonal. While the seasoned parties like the CPM and the CPI have a history of their own, with definite ideologies and committed cadres, the seasonal parties like the BSP, SP, NCP, etc. join the game only at the time of elections. The second category parties are formed by individuals professedly to serve this or that sectarian or regional cause by collecting floating cadres from different camps, finding uninvited candidates to contest the election. Whatever be the character and working of this colourful affair, its role in elections cannot be minimized. The seasoned parties, formed largely to serve the collective interests of the working classes, in general leave the business of elections to the bourgeois parties, showing scant interest in the elections where their strength is not solid.

The roles of the seasoned and seasonal parties are, thus, altogether different, seldom overlapping and always functioning within their respective fields that are far away from each other. While the ideology-oreinted parties of the communists remain involved in creating organizations of workers and farmers, students and teachers, landless labourers and regular employees, the election–orineted parties of the ambitious individuals set-up their shops at the right time just as the fast food stalls come up whenever and wherever some event is to take place. But the role of these small seasonal players cannot be minimized. At times, they act like the friendly or the hostile planets, making or marring the fortunes of those having high stakes in the gamble of power politics. As for the seasoned parties, their role is to force larger issues rather than coin catchy slogans as the agenda for the election. Not that they succeed in changing the character of the eletions, but they do drop among the electorate ideas that disturb at least the aware sections of society.

These parties that seem seasonal in Haryana asre serious parties elsewhere. As a matter of factr, the BSP, the NCP, the SP are all regional parties that have a strong base each in its own state of origin. They have also been forming governments in those states every now and then. The problem with these parties is that they aspire to become national parties, which perhaps is not a possibility, for there is an inherent opposition between the regional and the national. Whatever is regional cannot be national and whatever is national cannot be regional. Of course, from their position of strength in their own native state, they can get a share in the power at the Centre. Some of these parties are either members of the UPA or are supporting the UPA government headed by Dr. Manmohan Singh.

In Haryana, these parties have no stakes. It is only the ill-adjusted individuals from the major parties like the Congress and the BJP who persuade the heads of these regional outfits to open their sale counters in Haryana also. These sale counters are generally put up at the time of elections when candidates come calling for a ticket from any window. The parties do not have to spend on these stray condidtaes because they are wellversed in the art or craft of self-financing. In fact, these parties, if any thing, stand to gain; they receive "donations" for their organizations. Besides, they do get a certain percentage, however small, of the votes polled, which in turn would help them maintain their status in the Election Commission's list of political parties. Thus, these seasonal parties in one state but serious ones in some others have an important role to play in the maintenance of democaracy in this country. After all, the institution of democracy was created for giving an opportunity to each individual to form a party, to contest an election, and above all, to vote for a candidate and a party of one's choice. No wonder India is the largest democracy in the world, with the largest number of voters, the largest number of candidates, and the largets number of parties.

As for the seasoned political parties in Haryana, while the CPI, after its split in 1964, has remained only a poor cousin in the family of the communist parties, the CPM has stayed as a stable organization always active through its units doing special public jobs.

The Communist Party of India (Marxist) better known as CPM has had in Haryana a history longer than the history of Haryan itself. A contemporary of this author in terms of age, Comrade Dharam Singh Kasni from Dadri in district Bhiwani headed the organization in the years following the said split.

He used to edit a weekly which succeeded in securing a respectable number of subscribers. The weekly raised public issues and political anomalies, offering scathing criticism of the wrong govt. policies and programmes. Although a small band of activists, the cadres of CPM have always been known fro their courage of conviction. Its cadres are educated in the first place; even those without the benefit of formal education have political and economic awareness far better than the majority of the bourgeois parties can be credited with. One thing which the CPM sympathisers will consider a virtue, and its detractos would call a vice, is the party cadre's commitment to understanding and analysis.

No wonder, with its strong intellectual commitment, the CPM organization in Haryana devotes so much time to holding meetings and conferences, discussing and debating, analysing and understanding, the social developments and political trends of their time, especially those relating to the state of Haryana. While these exercises, continuously carried out, give the party cadres an added advantage, it also takes away the initiative for pratical activites of launching social movements or spearheading political struggle. Maybe a little magnified in the author's imagination, whenever he think of the CPM organization in Haryana, the case of Shakespeare's Hamlet comes to mind, the case as Coloridge, a poet-critic of the Bard in the Romantic age, viewed it. To cite the relevant part of the statement,

> Hamlet's character is the prevalence of the abstracting and generalizing habit over the practical. He does not want courage, skill, will, or opportunity, but every incident sets him thinking .... Hence great, enormous, intellectual activity and a consequent proportionate aversion to real action, with all its

> symptoms and accompanying qualities .... All mental forms being indefinite and ideal, realities must needs become cold, and hence it is the indefinite that combines with passion. (Coleridge, 158)

No other Indian political party can boast of such an intellectual orientation; no other party can also be so shy of mobilizing the masses. Perhaps in Haryana it has not been lucky in having a leader with a strong mass base, wholly involved in the populace. The next leading man of the CPM organization, after Comrade Dharam Singh Kasni, was Comrate Raghbir Singh Hooda, who made serious attempts to make some dent in the bourgeois politics by aligning with movements launched by leaders like Ch. Devi Lal. Comrade Hooda along with several of his team- mates, such as Comrade Pirthi Singh, Comrade Inderjit Singh, Comrade Balbir Singh Dahiya, etc., remained in jail for the entire period of the Emergency during 1975-77. Comrade Hooda also had a band of able lieutenants like Comrade Pirthi Singh, Comrade Inderjit Singh, Comrade Balbir Singh Dahiya, Comrade Sradhanad Solanki, who headed different front organizations of the party. All of these aging young men are still holding the party flag, doing their utmost to strike roots in the masses. But the status of the party does not seem to have improved so far as its mass contact is concerned. The average voter in Haryana remains unaware of their quiet intellectual work.

The CPM in Haryana has not been keen on contesting many seats in elections even to the state Assembly, leave aside elections to Parliament. Once or twice they secured a seat or two in the state Assembly with the support of Lok Dal headed by Ch. Devi Lal. Obviously, the party does not hope to play any decisive role in the power poltics of the state, being marginal in mass support. But the party has been able to make its presence felt in the student sector, where its student wing, the Student Federation of India (SFI), has been raising sensible issues of interest to students in particular and society in general. The party has also been brave in taking up issues most parties would choose to evade. The author can't help recalling here the case of Sushila's murder in Hisar in the 1980's, which the CPM alone showed the courage to it make a public issue.

Even more daring on the part of the CPM party was to take up the issue called the Revasa Kand during the Emergency. This was the time when people feared to discuss things even in their homes. But the courageous and fearless leaders of the party took up the case of a rural family that had been tortured, and most meanly dishonored, with a brother and a sister of the family forced to do what no brother and sister would ever wish to do. While most parties and persons of consequence observed silence, it were the leaders of the CPM, led by Comrade Pirthi Singh, who dared the lion in his den. Thus, the party may not have had any great role to play in the power poilitics of the state, its role in raising social issues cannot be underrated.

Also, if there is one political force in the state that enjoys an impeceable reputation for genuine secularism, it is the CPM. Through literature and pamphlets, seminars and symposia, demonstrations and confortations, it is this party that has consistently and continuously opposed all forms of casteism and communalism in the state. It may be the Hindu communalism or its opposite from the Muslims, or the Sikhs, the CPM in Haryana has always played a leading role in combating the virus of devisive politics. Though limited, the activism of the CPM in select areas has been unfailing. This party has always defended human rights and the civic liberties in Haryana – some political parties are not even aware of what these concepts mean.

The movement for people's democracy, while remaining in the back waters of the power politics, may result into a groundswell some day. With the market economy tightening its grip on the Indian political and social systems, it is but natural that the lower classes will be hit hard. And the harder the hit becomes, the greater will be the compulsions working upon the masses to seek a people's party like the CPM for resistence to the monster of Market Forces. Although the team of intelligent and committed leaders and reliable followers in the Haryana unit of the CPM is small in size, it is capable of taking up the challenge if the situation so warrants. Comrade Inderjit Singh, Comrade Pirthi Singh, Comrade Balbir Singh Dahiya and Comrade Sradha Nand Solanki are all poltical leaders of rare integrity and understanding,. They only need to move out to the masses, not nominally, nor sporadically, but on the state level and continuously, to seize the opportunity that seems to lie before them.

The opportunity that seems plausible is logical as well. The tighter the grip becomes of the ruthless market forces, the more compelling will become the life situation for the working classes, driving them out of their individualism and consumerism. In that do-or-die situation, the various opiums being used by the bourguois parties will prove utterly ineffective, leaving the masses disenchanted. Faced with the wolves of dire needs, the compulsions of survival in a Darwinion economy, the liquor of religions, of Ram Mandir, of caste and community's 'honour', would only burn the empty stomach, igniting a fire unextinguishable by any of these spurious drinks.

The CPM opportunity may be preceded by the BSP one, for in the immediate context, the latter seems to have better chances of attracting the 'poor' castes and communities. The caste-card still spells magic on the masses. Smt. Mayavati, carrying on the hard work done by Shri Kanshi Ram, seems to have felt the pulse of the toiling populace; she has struck it rich in U.P. And that has rightly made her ambitious. She would make a similar bid, using the same caste arithmetic, in Haryana and the other states that would go to polls in the next few years. Her politics is the same as practiced by the national parties such as the Congress and the BJP: Make the 'other' castes junior or subordinate partners. The Congress Party ruled for several decades using the lower castes as junior partners or subordinate supporters.

Smt. Mayavati has only reversed the equation. The ruling classes of yester years are now placed in junior, subordinate position; the higher castes are now replaced by the 'higher' numbers; the 'quantity' has taken over the 'quality', the quality of caste, the higher social status. Times are, for sure, changing, and changing for the better, weakening the centuries–old structure of feudalism, replacing it by the 'democracy of the proletariat'. Not a small change by any measure! And all as a result of one man's total commitment, and now one woman's determined fight against the guardians of the status- quo.

In a quick turn to the alternate available in the given situation, people had started talking of the return of Ch. Om Prakash Chautala in the next election, due in February 2010. But then came up the Bhajan Lal factor, with his younger son, Kuldip Bishnoi, voicing the dissent within the Congress, now from outside the party fold. Resenting the long spell of the 'Jat regime' beginning with Ch. Bansi Lal's term from 1996 to 1999, followed by Ch. Om Parkash Chautala's from 1999 to 2005, now being continued by the present term of Ch. Bhupinder Singh Hooda from 2005 to 2010 – the non-Jat castes and communities in the state are growing sick of the sameness; they are intensely itching for a change, a change seemingly favourable for the non-Jat castes.

This 'sickness of sameness', this 'intense itch for change', seems to favour the return of Ch. Bhajan Lal yet another time, reviving the old rotation system, as also the system of alternation between Ch. Bhajan Lal and Ch. Devi Lal or his son. Ch. Bhajan Lal's advantage is that he has been for long a symbol of the non-Jat forces in the state. Also, the BJP, which has been of late sore with Ch. Om Parkash Chautala's party (INLD), may happily join hands with the former. The Congress headed by Ch. Bhupinder Singh Hooda and the INLD of Ch. Om Parkash Chautala, in the popular non-Jat perception, are near allied, having for their support the common rural Jat voters.

Compared to the CPM movement for a people's democracy, the immediate prospect seems to be in favour of the Mayavati Movement, that can work in Haryana, too, just as it did in U.P., although Haryana is not quite the same as U.P. Working within the caste structure as also within the capitalist economy and expecting a radical change is to follow a hollow dream. Smt. Mayavati's only ambition is to capture power and then do in India as the Indians do. She certainly has no ideas beyond the bourgeois mechanics of grabbing power. And there she has been successful, sometimes partly, sometimes largely, and this time wholly in U.P., winning an absolute majority in the largest state of the Indian union, sixth nation in the world in terms of population.

Smt. Mayavati's ideology is typically bourguois. She works for seeking power through elections, just as any bourguois party does. She has never taken up any public issue, nor even launched nay movement for the poor and the deprived. Her focus always remains on using symbols and icons, overwhelm the mass imagination of her distinct electorate. She does all she can to sharpen the caste consciousness; the sharper the consciousness becomes, the greater is the polarization on caste lines. The various castes and communities in India feel satisfied if they have their own Chief Minister, their own District Magistrate, or their own Suprintendent of Police. The catch is that this 'tokenism' in social justice or political power-structure limits the benefits to a few, leaving out in the cold the large mass. And those out there in the cold cannot derive any pleasure from a distance, getting nothing much for their own subsistence. Consequently, things reach a dead end, breaking down the caste barriers, making minimum living conditions the common ground for an alliance between the poor, creating a formidable force of the have-nots. But that is a long historical process not reached in a day.The antagonized castes and communities remain divided socially, overriding economic differences within each caste.

When such a situation reaches, the relevance of the Communist Party is felt and a different form of polarization takes place, creating class rather than caste antagonism. The Communist Party in Haryana (the CPM), in the present phase, seems unable to make its presence felt. Despite there being frequent occurrence of situations like the one at Gurgoan, where violent confrontation came up in the Honda company between workers and employers, or the one at Karnal, where the Liberty Shoe Company forced its workers to launch a struggle for their rights. No doubt, it was only the CPM and its Front

Organizations that came out in support of the workers at both Gurgaon and Kanral, but the state unit's presence was not powerful enough to make an impact on the public perception. On both the occasions, national leaders of the CPM like Smt. Barinda Karat, the lone female member of the Party's Polit Bureau and wife of the Party's General Secretary, stole the show in the media. Of course, the local unit invites the national leaders, but an active organization does not push itself into the background, does not get lost into the general public offering resistance to the police atrocities. Once again, the key weakness of the state organization comes to mind – its inability to make its presence felt, to launch and spearhead mass movements. Everyday, we read reports of the general public protesting against the short supply of electricity, against the absence or failure of civic amenities, but we seldom find these protests articulated or spearheaded by the state organization of the CPM.

Maybe the situation calls for a change in the tactics and functioning of the CPM's Haryana unit. In any case, there seems a need for an urgent introspection on the part of the CPM's state unit, as to why it has not been able to make a breakthrough despite its having been there right from the days of the Freedom Struggle. Comparatively, it is doing better in Punjab, although even there it has not been able to improve its electoral gains. It seems the party takes pride in not being a purely election party like the BSP and all other bourgeois parties. But seen from another angle, one can also consider it yet another case of making virtue out of necessity. That is, if you are not in a position to put up candidates in the election, you can also say that you are not one of those bourguois outfits that spring into action only at the election time.

In the early years of the country's independence, the Communist Party did make such an attempt towards becoming an election party as well. But the result was not very encouraging; it attracted spurious stuff that defected to the ruling Congress party at the earliest opportunity, there being no stringent Anti-Defection Law in those days. We can recall here the elections of 1957 when Comrade Partap Singh Daulta with his famous red turban was elected to Parliament from Rohtak, Ch. Hukam Singh Dahiya was elected to the state Assembly from Rai. Then, there were others like Ch. Samsher Singh Surjewala, Ch. Randhir Singh, and several others who joined the party, but soon switched over to the Congress Party. Comrade Harpal Singh from Tohana was elected to the state Assembly in 1987, and so was Comrade Harnam Singh from Shahbad. This was with the help of Ch. Devi Lal's Lok Dal. These two have shown their steady commitment to the party, never succumbing to any temptation for securing a share, however small, in the power structure.

The Bahujan Samaj Party, on the other hand, is purely an election party, thriving, like any other regional outfit based on the vote–bank of a set of castes and communities sharing common social advantages or disadvantages. In its frantic search for power, the BSP has been wooing strange bed fellows, such as the BJP. The marriages of convenience which the BSP contracted three times proved disastrous on all the three occasions. It once tried some sort of understanding with the Congress Party as well, when the latter was a force in the state politics of U.P. After these failed experiments, the BSP contested alone. That, too, did not work. This time, in 2007, Smt. Mayawati tried a new experiment. She abandoned its hatred of the upper castes and decided to get wedded to the uppermost caste of Brahmins. With the Muslim votes always available to anyone in a position to defeat the BJP, the BSP had no problem in winning a majority on its own.

Whether the BSP would make a bid in the next Haryana Assembly election on the pattern it did in U.P. is not quite clear as yet, for the party has not yet sprung into action to that effect, although it has already announced candidates for five out of the ten seats for Parliament. But it has been contesting the Assembly elections in Haryana for over a quarter of a century, though without succeeding in becoming a major player. It had been only marking its presence in every election, by securing a small percentage of votes, and once or twice even succeeding in winning one or two seats. But if the BSP decides to seriously enter the election arena the next time, in the election due in February 2010, then there is a possibility that the expected alliance of Ch. Bhajan Lal and the BJP may work, just as the alliance of Ch. Bansi Lal's VHP and the BJP had worked in 1996. The entry of the BSP in its newly acquired form would make the contest four-cornered with the Congress Party, the INLD, the Bhajan Lal-BJP combine, and the BSP, all engaged in a grim battle for power. In that case, the contest may shift from the one between the Congress- and the INLD to that between the Bhajan Lal - BJP combine and the BSP. But in case the BJP decides to allign with INLD, then the chances become brighter for the latter.

All this may sound pure speculation. But the scenario to emerge in the next election due in 2010 seems to take shape on the lines speculated here. It may be too early to say in clear terms what precisely will be the political destiny of different parties aspiring to capture power in the state, but for the moment what has been speculated above seems a strong possibility. However, since the elctions in India are fought and won, not on ideological grounds, any sudden happeining, even raising of a catchy slogan, may tilt the scale in favour of one or the other contestant. For a more clear picture to emerge it may take two more years, for it is only on the eve of the election that permutations and combinations of different parties mature and the clouds start clearing to show which side the wind would blow. The byelection of May 22, 2008 to the three Assembly seats will certainly give some signals about the general election to follow.

Thus, the expected or desired shift from power politics to the poltics of the poor may take a long time to come. In the interim period, the bourgeois battle will continue, keeping principled and value-based poltics at bay. The centuries old social and political structures cannot be wished away, nor easily reshaped. But the fast changing social and economic conditions are bound to force a weakening of these structures, making the lower castes and classes more assestive if not more militant, increasingly tilting the rural-urban demography in favour of the latter, compelling the political focus more and more on secular concerns in place of the communal and the casteist. The last is bound to take place under the increasing pressure of globalisation and consumerism, both being secular in character, averse to adopting any other value than the one based on profit-making.

As things stand today, the chances for a secular politics, based on economic issues rather than those derived from interests of castes and communities, seem quite strong. However, whether the Communist, Socialist and Liberal groups and parties will be able to take advantage of the situation, only time will tell. Whether the situation is not yet ripe, or the CPM is not yet prepared for an intervention, the party needs to decide for itself and do the needful. But the situation does call for a collaboration of all these elements to take advantage of the situation shaping at the present time. If the intellectualism of the CPM and its possible allies can also accommodate activism, they are sure to expand the ground beneath their feat, expanding their field of activity and area of influence. Thus, the near and the far prospects of Haryana politics that we have tried to project here are only pointers, and not prophesies, of things to come. Much will depend upon the measures the leadership in each party initiates and pursnes during the period of two years left before the next election in 2010. The only thing that can be said at the moment is that the battle this time will be more tough than ever before for all those wanting to make a bid for capturing power in the state.

15

Some Inferences

Concluding our history of sorts of power politics in Haryana, some inferences seem unavoidable, some interpretations inevitable. An obvious inference is that the politics of Haryana has been dominated by certain families that came to prominence in the early years of the twentieth century, with only one or two exceptions that rose from nowhere. Some of these influential families, active in the game of power politics, grew into prominence after independence in 1947, and one or two still later after the formation of Haryana in 1966. All the same, the game of Haryana's power politics has been a privileged activity of a handful of families.

Among these power-oriented leading families, while Rao Birender Singh's seems to have the longest past, going back into the nineteenth century, and even before, those of Ch. Bhupinder Singh Hooda, Ch. Om Parkash Chautala and Ch. Birender Singh came to prominence in the early 20th century. The last, in fact, came up only because related to Ch. Chhotu

Ram, whereas the other two came up as rivals to Ch. Chhotu Ram's politics of collaboration. The families of Ch. Bansi Lal and Ch. Bhajan Lal are comparatively younger in power politics and came up only after trhe formation of Haryana in 1966.

Here we need to look a little further into the growth of these families in the arena of politics, as also to ponder why others with different backgrounds could not consolidate their position to acquire the prestigious status of the noted families. Those who came to dominate Haryana politics were mostly the ones who had become prominent at the time of Haryana's adoption of the Arya Samaj movement and its participation in the freedom movement. Both the families of Ch. Bhupinder Singh Hooda and of Ch. Om Parkash Chautala participated in the Arya Samaj movement as well as the freedom movement, emerging in their respective regions as the leading families among the Jats.

But there are glaring exceptions; like the families of Ch. Bansi Lal and Ch. Bhajan Lal. They came into prominence from humble backgroiund, and only after the formation of Haryana. These two families, surprisingly, ruled the state for about a quarter of a century. This is quite a long period in view of the fact that Haryana is only a little over forty years of age. An important factor in the rise of all these families to political prominence has been caste. Whereas all the long-time players have been from the Jat community, others, including Ch. Bhajan Lal, have been from the rural base. No Chief Minister of Haryana, including Pandit Bhagwat Dayal Sharma, had an urban background.

Why could not any family from the Scheduled and Backward castes attain that status of the noted family, despite there being senior leaders from these castes, some of them contemporaries of the three Lals? These leaders include Ch. Chand Ram and Ch. Dalbir Singh. Neither of these two tall Dalit leaders could make it to the top position of the Chief Minister. Both had long political careers, contesting many a time elections to both Parliament and State Assemblies, becoming Ministers both in the Union Cabinet as well as the State Governments.

There have been senior politicians after these two stalwarts, such as Ch. Phool Chand Mullana, Ch. Shyam Chand, Smt. Kartar Devi, Smt Shakuntala Bhagwaria, all of whom have been MLA's and Ministers several times in the state, but none of them could grow to the status of a leader nor did their families turn into Khandans or noted families. Others from the Dalit castes included Shri Ram Parkash, Phool Chand Dhanak and Amar Singh Dhanak, who, too, had long spans in politics.

There are some cases where the second generation, son or daughter, got a chance to enter politics. One such case is that of Kumari Selja. Her father, Ch. Dalbir Singh, had a long political career both in the State Assembly and at the Centre, and his brother Ch. Neki Ram had remained MLA for more than one term. Another case is that of Ch. Gaya Lal of Hodal in Faridabad, whose son now is an MLA. At least Ch. Chand Ram and Ch. Dlabir Singh qualified for the top position, but they were never given any opportunity to reach that goal.

Except for the family of Ch. Dalbir Singh, none other of the scheduled caste leaders acquired any status or position to maintain prominence in the power politics of Haryana. With Kumari Selja not yet married, although she has been M.P. and Minister more than once, the family does not seem to have very bright chances of continuing its position through future generations. In fact, from Ch. Dalbir Singh to Kumari Selja, there is already some diminishing of the family status in the power politics of the state.

One can notice the dominant role of the cast structure operating in the fact that despite these Scheduled Caste politicians having credentials of an elite education and long political experience, they have never been in a position to dominate state politics. None from these castes has ever held the top position in the state Cabinet.

The case of the Backward Castes is no better. None from these castes has ever held the highest position in the Cabinet or in the party organization. In fact, even in the Cabinet, their position, if ever, has been nominal. The one who reached nearest to the highest position is Dr. Ram Parkash from Kurukshetra, who for a while held the position of the Working President of the State Congress Committee. But the fact that he could retain the position only for a few months proves the weak position of the OBC's in the power structure of the state. Like Ramji Lal before him, Dr. Ram Parkash has been elected to Rajya Sabha.

Ch. Phool Chand Mullana is perhaps the first President of the Haryana Congress, thanks to the threat the Congress senses from the rising influence of Smt. Mayavati among the Dalit castes. Ch. Dalbir Singh did, of course, occupy that position once, but his span was too short to remain in the people's memory.

The case of women is similar to that of these weaker castes. Women being another disadvantaged section of our society, they have never got a chance to head the government or the party in the state, although there have been important women politicians even before the formation of Haryana. Two of them, Smt. Parasani Devi and Behen Cahanderavati, are still in active poltics, both of whom were elected to the State Assembly in the early 1950's, whereas Ch. Bansi Lal, Ch. Bhajan Lal and Ch. Bhupinder Singh Hooda (all have been Chief Ministers of Haryana) started their political careers in the 1960s or later.

Also, despite the fact that both Behen Chanderavati and Smt. Parsani Devi come from Jat families, they never got a chance to head the state government or the political organization. Besides, there have been other promionent women politicians, such as Smt.Om Prabha Jain of Kaithal, who is no more, and Smt. Sharda Rani of Ballabgarh, a Rajput by caste. Both remained Ministers in Ch. Bansi Lal's Cabinet.

All of these women, like the leaders of the Scheduled Castes, have to their credit a good education and have maintained decent personal records even in the murky politics of Haryana. And yet, none of these women, like none of the leaders of lower castes, ever got a chance to rise to prominent party or governmental positions, nor could they develop their families into *khandans*. With none of their junior family members in line to continue the political lineage, there seems no chance for their families to emerge influential.

One good thing about the politics of Haryana has been that it has not had any inglorious record of communalism. No doubt, there was large scale communal violence in 1947, caused by the country's partition. There has been a significant change since the formation of the state in 1966, compared to the states like Gujrat, U.P, Madhya Pradesh and Rajasthan, where communal violence has been taking place every now and then. One reason, of course, is that in Haryana the Muslim population is not very large, and whatever is there is concentrated, largely, in a segment of the state.

That may also be the reason why the BJP could not get a strong foothold in the state, although it carries considerable influence in the towns, especially among the Punjabi Hindus. There is, no doubt, a sizeable population of the Sikhs in Haryana spread all along the breadth of the state bordering Punjab. It is creditable that despite repeated provocations by the extremists in Punjab during the 1980's, no communal violence took place even in this belt. There were only stray incidents in one or two towns after the assassination of Smt. Indira Gandhi in 1984.

Why the state has had a comparatively better record of communal harmony is perhaps because of the role Ch. Chhotu Ram had played in bringing together the peasants of different castes and communities. Also, all those leaders who had spearheaded in the state the Arya Samaj movement and the Freedom Movement played an equally important role in creating an atmosphere of social harmony.

Ch. Chhotu Ram's political position was, however, at variance with his social position. In the social setup the Jat leader was a staunch Arya Samajist, and as such was totally against cow slaughter. In the business of cow slaughter, not only the Muslims but also the Hindus of lower castes were involved for reasons of livelihood. Obviously, Ch. Chhotu Ram always supported the cow-protectors who at times would even kill those suspected of cow-slaughtering.

Despite this dichotomy, however, Ch. Chhotu Ram had greatly contributed towards maintaining communal harmony in Punjab (Haryana in his time formed a part of Punjab). Thus, while he was a great friend of the Muslims in political life, he was a great opponent to them as enemies of the cow. Fortunately, cow slaughter, if any, has not caused any communal violence in Haryana since its formation in 1966; in fact, not since Independence.

Another factor responsible for communal harmony in Haryana has been the absence of religious fanaticism among the dominant peasant castes and the lower castes in Haryana. It is only among the upper castes in the urban centers that a feeling for institutionalized religion has been strong. But the record of the last forty years of the state shows fairly encouraging signs that the scope for communal violence is considerably reduced.

Also considerably reduced has become the antagonism between the rural and the urban populations, which at one time had emerged as a major political plank. It was on this very plank that Ch. Chhotu Ram had emerged as a great leader of the peasantry in unpartioned Punjab. One of the reasons for the reduction in that antagonism has been the expansion of the urban sector, more and more people moving to urban settlements, with even the villages getting urbanized in life style, owing largely to the introduction of technologies, such as the T.V., the mobile, and owing also to rapid commercialization.

The gap in the life style of the urban and the rural populations is now getting narrower, although the same may not be true of the gap between the two economics. As a matter of fact, the gap now is not so much horizontal as vertical. The gap between the rich and the poor, in the town and the village alike, is decidedly widening. Consequently, polarities of politics are also bound to undergo some changes. But that stage does not seem to have been reached as yet.

The contest for power in Haryana, however, is still restricted to those representing the rural elite. Even if they have been living in the towns or the megacities, their identification remains with the rural castes and communities, one or the other, and the castes and communities, too, do not disown them as their leaders. The rural origin of these leaders continues to help them maintain their rural identity.

The strong hold in Haryana of the traditional structure of castes and communities, and of the joint family system, is also borne out by the fact that despite there being half the electoral population of young men and women, a large majority of whom possessing at least school education, these young men and women still identify themselves with their families, their castes, and communities, one way or another, when it comes to electing representatives to the democratic institutions. Independent youth power, free from the bonds of family and caste ties, is yet to take shape in the state of Haryana.

The case of women is still worse. They are yet to acquire their own individual identities, as their votes are almost taken for granted by their fathers and husbands. In other words, in most cases, it is the families, not the individuals, that decide the electoral fortunes. Despite all the laws recently enacted for the protection of women and their rights, they continue to live as appendages to their families, before as well as after marriage. Very few women, especially in the villages, independently exercise their franchise.

There does seem to have come about an improvement in reducing malpractices in the elections, thanks to the proactive role of the Election Commission of India. The introduction of electronic machines for voting in place of ballot papers, and of identity cards in place of 'verification-on-objection' practice, have decidedly reduced bogus voting to a large extent. Besides, the increasing participation of the security forces drawn from the Central pool has also helped in reducing the role of muscle power.

The money power, of course, still continues to play an important role, for all compartments of the election mechanism have been affected by the increasing commercialism in our time. From lobbying for securing the party ticket to organizing the election campaign for creating a favourable climate to finally ensuring the actual polling of votes, those in the electoral battle have to spend lacs and crores of rupees to make it to the Assembly or the Parliament.

Over the years, those believing in earning by the sweat of their brow have been eliminated from contesting an election, any election, from the village Panchayat to the national Parliament. No wonder the first thing those elected at any level of the democratic pyramid do is to make tons of money so that they can sustain themselves in the tough business of politics. Hence a small class of people remains privileged to carry the burden of democracy in the state.

In the matter of political parties, Haryana has not seen the entry of many new formations since the earliest phase of its politics, largely defined by Ch. Chhotu Ram. It is the same Congress Party versus the Zamindar League or the Lok Dal or the Indian National Lok Dal that remain the major contestants for power, with the Jan Sangh or the BJP remaining the third player.

The leadership in the two main contending parties continues to stay with the leaders carrying rural identities, but only with those who have risen far above the rest, much above the rural folk in all respects: wealth or education. If any one in either of the two parties grows oversize, he is eased out sooner than later by whoever is in control of things.

The control in the case of the INLD, of course, remains stable, there being no scope for any individual or family to replace the founding family. If there is any power struggle in the party, it remains confined among the members of that family. Others would not dare even to think of staging any coup in that party. There seems no chance of reaching that stage in the near future.

As for the Congress Party, the control cannot remain stable. As a matter of policy, the High Command keeps changing its state leaders, making sure that no one becomes indispensable. But the individuals who get more than one chance to hold the control of the state government of the Congress Party naturally start considering themselves indispensable. And the moment such individuals are replaced by a new controller, they feel uneasy, start behaving individually, leaving no option for the Party but to show them the door. Ch. Bansi Lal met that fate. And now Ch. Bhajan Lal is on the same path.

Another clear inference about the power politics in Haryana is that the game continues to be traditional, call it feudal, with the political parties representing the interests of various castes and communities whose permutations and combinations alone determine the electoral fortunes of the political parties as well as the contesting individuals. Those political parties that are formed on the basis of ideologies, mainly the CPI and the CPM in Haryana, are yet to gain any ground in the game of power politics.

Even the Hindu Nationalism of the BJP carries no appeal with the rural masses of Haryana. Whatever place it has for long occupied in the state has been possible because of its being a representative of the interests of a community, the community of the Punjabi-speaking people who had to migrate from East Punjab, now the deominant province of Pakistan.

Despite all the modernization, commercialization, and globalization, the social structure and hence the political structure in Haryana, as well as in the country at large, continues to remain caste and community based. We are a congregation of castes and communities, be it a society or a nation. While our economic life is wholly managed individually, our political life is governed to a large extent by our castes and communities.

Yet another noticeable feature in Haryana's power politics is that while the politicians are turning to business, the businessmen are turning to politics. We know how Ch. Om Parkash Chautala, Ch. Bhajan Lal, Ch. Bansi Lal, Rao Birender Singh, Ch. Jai Parkash, etc., have all turned to business, perhaps finding that to be the only way to invest, and expect returns to, their earnings. At the same time, Shri Om Parkash Jindal, Shri Vinod Kumar Sharma, Shri Ramesh Kumar Gupta, Shri Mange Ram Gupta, Shri Balbir Pal Shah, and several more are essentially businessmen. They find their business helped by their being members of Parliament or the State Assembly. Over the years, the number of these conversions from politics to business and from business to politics has increased manyfold and it remains on the rise.

It is an indication of the stranglehold of tradition on the society in Haryana that despite the tremendous rise of education among women in recent years, the number of women legislators continues to be stable at less than ten percent of the total strength of 90 in the state Assembly. It is just about the same in the Parliament. At present, we have one woman M.P. out of ten from the state. At times, even this one is not there.

In view of this sad fact about the political status of women, there are strong reasons in favour of reservation for women in elections to the state Assemblies and the Parliament. We know how readily the proposal for 33% reservation for women in the village Panchayats was accepted, but how reluctantly the bill proposing the same reservation in the Assemblies and the Parliament was introduced, and how cleverly and cunningly, with all the quibbles of propriety and procedure, it is being kept pending for several years now. No wonder the game of power politics in Haryana, as well as in the country at large, continues to be an exclusively male preserve.

There is also a need for the reservation of seats in the State Assemblies as well as the national Parliament for the youth, young men and women below the age of 30 or 35. As of today, there are very few young men and women in these Houses of power. There are a few, but they are there to represent certain privileged families, not the youth of this country. Shri Madho Rao Scindia's son, Shri. Rajesh Pilot's son, or Farooq Abdulla's son or Ch. Dalbir Singh's daughter are in Parliament because their fathers happened to be privileged persons.

Even otherwise, important leaders continue having a share in the power structure. The political parties also maintain their positions of power through influenctial families. Seikh

Abdulas son, Shri Mulayam Singh's son, Shri. Karuna Nidhi's son, Shri Bal Thakarey's son, Sardar Parkash Singh Badal's son, Smt. Vasundra Raje Scindia's son, all have to carry on the political "responsibilities" of their respective families.

Back home in Haryana, two ministers of Ch. Bhupinder Singh Hooda's Cabinet, Ch. Sureinder Singh and Shri Om Parkash Jindal died in an air crash very unfortunately. Both were soon replaced by their wives. The instant emotional appeal helps the political parties to win Assembly or Parliament seats. Even otherwise, a son or a brother, a daughter or a wife, from the family is an additional advantage to the lineage in the consortium of ruling families. Ch. Samsher Singh Surjewala's son, Ch. Bhajan Lal's two sons, Ch. Om Parkash Chautala's both the sons, Rao Birender Singh's sons, Ch. Bansi Lal's son, son-in-law, and daughter in law, Ch. Bhupinder Singh Hooda's son, Ch. Jai Parkash's brother (his son is not of age yet), all are there in politics to maintain their membership of the ruling elite.

If the feudal structure of our society is to be replaced by a genuine democratic structure, then reservation for the youth will be a step in that direction. Of course, these powerful families will easily manage to induct more of their sons and daughters in the name of youth. That calls for the restructuring of our political parties as well, which are not really democratic, While most regional parties are like the private limited businesses of each family controlling such an outfit, the bourgeois national parties rely upon the traditional caste and community combinations represented by the influential families of each component. The Congress Party in particular practises this pattern, basically drawn from the Pre-Independence feudal model. The BJP does not rely on the family lineage, but the hold of the old guards and the back-seat driving by the RSS leaves no scope for a genuine democratic set up in the party. How the political parties can be genuimely democratic is a long and hard task a difficult to discus within the limited scope of the present book.

One way of ensuring representation to the different classes of modern, secular societies–or in order to make them so–is to fix representations occupation-wise, rather than caste or community-wise. The known professions like farming, landless labour, organized labour in the industry, unorganized labour in the domestic sector, teachers and lawyers, secretarial staff, etc., can be given representation by creating constituencies in keeping with their respective numerical strength. At least for a time, new leadership will emerge based on the professional basis, not on the basis of family lineage or business status, or caste strength. This will certainly take us a step forward from the centuries-old feudal structure of outr society.

A comparatively elitist model of modern representation is the one being followed in Germany, where 50 percent seats in Parliament are filled through open election, each party then getting the same number of seats it has won through open election for the nomination of intellectuals and professionals drawn from different fields of activity. The disadvantage of this system is that the larger political parties have the greater power of nomination, not necessarily ensuring representation of all sections of the working classes or professionals. Still, it does ensure representation to those not in the business of politics.

One of the steps urgently required to be taken is to strengthen the school system in the rural sector, which at present is very weak. Also, each village must be provided with a public library of a considerable size so that the village folk can have some life of the mind. This may not show instant results, but in the long run it will help transform village societies into modern settlements. Yet another, and equally or more important, step is to convert villages into mini towns, with all the amenities available in the urban settlements. It is owing to the absence of these modern amenities in our villages that all those posted in the rural sector–teachers, doctors, and others–prefer to stay in the cities even while working in the viilages, some even sacrificing their jobs rather than remain posted in the villages.

Once modern amenities are provided in the villages, and the educated classes of professionals start living there, village culture will undergo a sea change. And that change will decidedly change the character of our politics; it will help transform our feudal politics to the secular politics of modern socities. This new form of politics, we know, is determined not by caste or community vote, but by class and professional interests. In fact, the new form of politics will be based on economic and political ideologies rather than caste and community affiliations. Those who are interested in the modernization of Haryana, including its politics, need to work in this direction.

Works Cited

Chapter One:

Dutta, Nonika. *Forming Identity: A Social History of the Jats.* New Delhi: Oxford University Press, 1999.

Juneja, M.M. and Kulbir Singh Mor (eds.). *The Diaries of Dr Ram Ji Lal Hooda.* Hisar: Modern Book Co., 1989.

Malik, Shiva N. *Seth Chhaju Ram: A Life With a Purpose.* Hisar: Aman Parkashan, 1994.

Narain, Jagat. *Reports of India Election Petitions, Vol. II (1923-25).* Calcutta: Eastern Law House, 1930.

Chapter Two:

Singh, Dr Ranjit. *Professor Sher Singh: Ek Prerik Vyakti.* Rohtak : The Professor Sher Singh Abhinandan Samiti, 1991. Most incidents related to Professor Sher Singh are based on the contents of Dr Singh's book.

Chapter Three:

Harrison, G.B. *Shakespeare: The Complete Works.* New York: Harcourt, Brace & World. Inc., 1968.

Singh, Dr Ranjit. *Professor Sher Singh: Ek Prerik Vyakti.* Rohtak : The Professor Sher Singh Abhinandan Samiti, 1991.

Chapter Four:

Harrison, G.B.(Ed.) *Shakespeare: The Complete Works.* New York: Harcourt, Brace & World. Inc., 1968.

Singh, Dr Ranjit. *Professor Sher Singh: Ek Prerik Vyakti.* Rohtak : The Professor Sher Singh Abhinandan Samiti, 1991.

Chapter Six:

Desai, R.W. (Ed.). *Johnson on Shakespeare.* New Delhi: Orient Longman, 1979.

Chapter Seven:

Harrison, G.B. (Ed.). *Shakespeare: The Complete Works.* New York: Harcourt, Brace & World. INC.

Steinbeck, John. *In Dubious Battle.* London: Pan, 1936.

Chapter Nine:

Harrison, G.B. (Ed.). *Shakespeare: The Complete Works.* New York: Harcourt, Brace & World. Inc., 1968.

Chapter Ten:

Eliot, T.S. *The Waste Land and Other Poems.* London: Faber and Faber, 1923.

Chapter Fourteen:

Coleridge, S.T. *Coleridge on Shakespeare.* Ed. Terence Hawkes. Middlesex: Penguin Books, 1969.

Index

W

Y

Z